We know firsthand that marriage certainly isn't a journey filled only wit[h] full of storms, tears, heartache, and loss. Jeremy and Adrienne remind u[s] marriage can be by also addressing the hard and messy parts we must dig through to get there.

—MARY BETH and STEVEN CURTIS CHAPMAN

Reading *In Unison* is like being welcomed into Jeremy and Adie's living room and into their hearts! With authenticity these dear friends of mine share stories from their lives while simultaneously inviting a sense of community through their book. Prepare to encounter encouragement, practical help for your relationship, and always Jesus' hope!

—REBECCA ST. JAMES, singer and author

Jeremy and Adrienne are an inspiring example of putting the hard work into what matters. They graciously share the precious stones mined from their good times and bad times. No matter what season you're in or headed toward, *In Unison* will be life-giving to you!

—LEVI LUSKO, lead pastor of Fresh Life Church and bestselling author

Jeremy and Adie have a beautiful marriage centered around Jesus. I have personally witnessed the way they love and laugh and live together. Read it with your spouse!

—KAREN KINGSBURY, #1 *New York Times* bestselling author of *Someone Like You*

Jeremy and Adie's story is just like them—fun, fresh, and full of surprises. There is a rare authenticity that wafts through their atmosphere. You will find their journey refreshing and impossible to put down.

—SKIP HEITZIG, pastor and author

Jeremy and Adrienne's love for Jesus and each other is something to be emulated, and their marriage and friendship is one worth exploring and mining for gold.

—JONATHAN PITTS, executive pastor, Church of the City, and president, For Girls Like You Ministries

In Unison is a handbook for couples (and even singles in preparation) who desire to build a Christ-centered relationship. The wisdom that Jeremy and Adrienne offer through their experience with Christ and each other is undeniably valuable!

—KEVIN DOWNES, Kingdom Story Company producer, actor, director, and writer

This book is our new go-to gift for married couples of any age! Jeremy and Adie paint a beautiful picture of marriage. It's real, it's raw, it's *relatable*, it's hilarious, and it leaves you emboldened to fight for marriage, knowing that it's possible only with Jesus at its core.

—SCOTT and MELISSA REEVES, daytime actors

Jeremy and Adie Camp are dearly loved friends who are both personal and professional inspirations to me and my family. *In Unison* is written on the foundation of what I have witnessed them living out in their daily lives.

—ANTHONY EVANS, worship leader and recording artist

In Unison is one of the best marriage books we have read, and we have been married for 41 years. Jeremy and Adrienne write about their marriage with refreshing honesty, humor, and wisdom from God's Word.

—PASTOR JOE and CATHY FOCHT, Calvary Chapel of Philadelphia

In Unison is a true gift. Jeremy and Adrienne Camp graciously share some of the most intimate building blocks of their successful marriage. They share their own unique experiences in a way that is conversational and relatable, but at all times woven together to be a beautiful story of oneness.

EJ GAINES, vice president of marketing, Capitol CMG

In Unison brilliantly combines the honest details of Jeremy's and Adie's marriage and the scriptural principles that are helpful for every marriage. Readers will come away with treasures for their own marriage.

—JANICE GAINES, national recording artist and speaker

The wisdom on the pages of *In Unison* can change the story of your marriage. Your life—and the life of your spouse—will be made all the better for the insight and grace that the Camps pour out from their own love story. Don't miss this book!

—JONATHAN ALLEN, worship pastor, Grace Chapel, and ALLISON ALLEN, author and speaker

IN UNISON

JEREMY AND ADRIENNE CAMP

WITH AMANDA HOPE HALEY

HARVEST HOUSE PUBLISHERS
EUGENE, OREGON

In Unison
Copyright © 2020 by Jeremy and Adrienne Camp
Published by Harvest House Publishers
Eugene, Oregon 97408
www.harvesthousepublishers.com

ISBN 978-0-7369-8068-5 (pbk.)
ISBN 978-0-7369-8069-2 (eBook)

Library of Congress Control Number: 2019956334

Printed in the United States of America

20 21 22 23 24 25 26 27 28 / VP-FO / 10 9 8 7 6 5 4 3 2 1

To the ones who paved the way for us:

OUR PARENTS, TOM AND TERI CAMP AND RORY AND WENDY LIESCHING,

among whom there is a collection of over 85 years of marriage.

Way to go, guys!

And to the ones to whom we're handing the baton:

EGAN, ARIANNE, AND ISABELLA.

May you never forget Jesus as your first love, and may

His life flow through all you do.

Since we are surrounded by such a great cloud of witnesses, let us throw off everything that hinders and the sin that so easily entangles. And let us run with perseverance the race marked out for us, fixing our eyes on Jesus, the pioneer and perfecter of faith.

HEBREWS 12:1-2 NIV

CONTENTS

WHY WE WROTE THIS BOOK

We want to share some of what we have learned about marriage and who we are as individuals. This is not all of our story, nor does this book include every detail of our lives—but we hope it gives you a good look into who we are and what our marriage is like as we try to follow God's will in often unusual circumstances. The advice we share is not meant to address severe marital issues (there are gifted, godly counselors for that!), and this is not a we-have-it-all-together book, because we don't. This is about how having Jesus in the center of our lives is the most effective and fulfilling way to live. After 17 years together, we love being married, and we recognize that alone is a huge victory.

We hope you will be inspired to build and sow into your marriage. It will produce a harvest well worth reaping!

MEET ADRIENNE

FULL NAME?

Adrienne Elizabeth Camp, née Liesching

BIRTH DATE?

July 12, 1981

BIRTHPLACE?

Port Elizabeth, South Africa

NICKNAME?

Adie (that's pronounced Ay-dee, like Sadie!), Adrie, or Ades

ARE YOU USUALLY EARLY OR LATE?

Early or right on time

PETS?

Yes—dogs, chickens, fish

BOOKS OR E-BOOKS?

Books, for sure. I love the smell and turning the pages.

FAVORITE FOOD?

Middle Eastern food and sushi

FAVORITE MOVIE?

Any superhero movie

FAVORITE SCRIPTURE?

"I have been crucified with Christ. It is no longer I who live, but Christ who lives in me" (Galatians 2:20).

MOST INTERESTING PLACE YOU'VE BEEN?

I've been privileged to travel to many different places, but I would probably say Israel. The history, food, and culture never get old to me. I could go back there a hundred times.

BEST VACATION DESTINATION?

Saint John, US Virgin Islands

HOW MANY LANGUAGES DO YOU SPEAK?

Two fluently (English and Afrikaans), a small amount of Arabic, and an even smaller amount of Xhosa

WHAT DO YOU WANT YOUR EPITAPH TO BE?

"She gave everything she had."

WHAT IS SOMETHING YOU WILL NEVER DO AGAIN?

Eat oysters

WHAT DO YOU WISH YOUR BRAIN WERE BETTER AT DOING?

Remembering people's names

HAVE YOU EVER SAVED SOMEONE'S LIFE?

I pulled our son, Egan, out of the pool once.

WHICH OF YOUR SCARS HAS THE BEST STORY BEHIND IT?

I have a small scar on my forehead from running into a stationary World War II airplane propeller in a museum. I knocked myself out and woke up in my dad's arms, covered in blood, with everyone praying for me.

WHAT'S YOUR FAVORITE THING ABOUT YOUR SPOUSE?

His passion for everything he does. He is extreme in whatever he's doing, and he challenges me in the best of ways.

IF YOUR CHILDHOOD HAD A SMELL, WHAT WOULD IT BE?

Definitely the beach. I grew up in sunny South Africa, along the ocean.

WHAT IS YOUR FAVORITE PART OF MARRIAGE?

Getting to experience life—the ups and downs—with my best friend. I agree with Solomon 100 percent when he said, "Two are better than one" (Ecclesiastes 4:9).

MEET JEREMY

FULL NAME?

Jeremy Thomas Camp

BIRTH DATE?

January 12, 1978

BIRTHPLACE?

Lafayette, Indiana

NICKNAME?

I have a ton: Jerm, Jerminator, Jermany, and JT, to name a few.

ARE YOU USUALLY EARLY OR LATE?

On time or a little late

PETS?

We have two dogs. I like one of them.

BOOKS OR E-BOOKS?

Kindle, for sure—you can take as many books as you want with you, and it hardly weighs a thing!

FAVORITE FOOD?

East Indian food and sushi

FAVORITE MOVIE?

Nacho Libre and *Les Misérables*

FAVORITE SCRIPTURE?

"I do not account my life of any value nor as precious to myself, if only I may finish my course and the ministry that I received from the Lord Jesus, to testify to the gospel of the grace of God" (Acts 20:24).

MOST INTERESTING PLACE YOU'VE BEEN?

I've been to 42 countries and loved all of them, but I'd say the Faroe Islands stand out the most to me. That area is one of the most beautiful and fascinating places I have visited. They still eat whale blubber. No thanks!

BEST VACATION DESTINATION?

Saint John, US Virgin Islands

HOW MANY LANGUAGES DO YOU SPEAK?

English and a very little bit of Spanish

WHAT DO YOU WANT YOUR EPITAPH TO BE?

"In everything he did, he lived wholeheartedly for the Lord."

WHAT IS SOMETHING YOU WILL NEVER DO AGAIN?

Eat whale blubber

WHAT DO YOU WISH YOUR BRAIN WERE BETTER AT DOING?

Shutting off at night

HAVE YOU EVER SAVED SOMEONE'S LIFE?

I haven't, but I would jump in a heartbeat if a situation ever called for it.

WHICH OF YOUR SCARS HAS THE BEST STORY BEHIND IT?

I have a scar on the side of my head from when I was two years old and climbed onto a table (probably to sneak candy) and came tumbling down.

WHAT'S YOUR FAVORITE THING ABOUT YOUR SPOUSE?

Her sensitivity to the things of the Lord. She constantly checks her heart in circumstances and yields quickly to God's heart behind them.

IF YOUR CHILDHOOD HAD A SMELL, WHAT WOULD IT BE?

Fresh wind and bike tires from when I would ride my BMX bicycle

WHAT IS YOUR FAVORITE PART OF MARRIAGE?

I get to live this journey that God has placed me on with my best friend.

— I —

NOT

MY TYPE

Jeremy and I met in September 2002 while we were both on a tour called Festival Con Dios with about ten other bands. Before the tour started, I chatted with one of my friends who worked at our record label, expressing my disappointment in how few godly men I thought there were—or at least who hadn't yet been taken. I had toured with many great guys over the years who all became my friends, and I expected this was going to be no different.

She mentioned I was about to meet a special one on this upcoming tour.

This guy, Jeremy Camp, had withstood the devastating trial of watching his young wife pass away from cancer, and he was one of the sweetest, godliest guys she had ever met.

I was vaguely familiar with Jeremy through the music industry, but since I was into a completely different style of music than his, I adamantly responded, "Oh no, I've heard his music. And he's definitely not my type."

I was convinced I would marry a visual artist—a painter, sculptor, or photographer—perhaps tall, skinny, and oozing creativity. I also had the youthful notion that in order to marry someone, I had to enjoy pretty much all the same things as him. Oh, and since I am from South Africa, I had vowed never to marry an American. (I had a misconception about our cultural differences and wanted to stay as connected to South Africa as possible.) So post-grunge, athletic, American Jeremy did not fit my description of the guy I thought I wanted.

I had only ever dated one person, and although it was a silly, brief relationship, it had a bit of a messy ending from which I was still feeling emotional effects and insecurities. All I wanted was to throw myself fully into Jesus. I certainly didn't want a new distraction in my life after all the restorative work the Lord had been doing in my heart.

Early into the outdoor tour through 40-plus cities, I sprained my ankle quite badly trying to

THE BENJAMIN GATE

escape a torrential downpour. I ended up having to play my shows while wearing a huge ankle brace for a couple weeks, much to my dismay. As the front woman of a passionate rock band, The Benjamin Gate, it wasn't my style to be hindered. I believed you had to leave your heart bleeding on the stage when you walked off, and if I couldn't do that, then I didn't feel as if I had done my job properly.

Shortly after my fall, Jeremy introduced himself to me and told me that he and his band had prayed for me the day before. I was surprised but encouraged, and I mentioned to him that we had a mutual friend at the record label.

That was it. No sparks. No flame. No further thought.

But I realized Jeremy was very kind and more tender than most people I had met, and it was evident he had a deep relationship with the Lord.

THE HOTEL STRANGER

Our merchandise tables were providentially set up near each other's, so over the course of the next three months we saw each other and had some form of interaction every day. Typically while touring, especially during festival season, I'd head to the hotel for a shower after the show was finished before hitting the road and traveling to the next venue.

On one occasion I was hobbling toward my hotel room, still wearing my gigantic ankle brace, when a guy standing in the hallway greeted me. Thinking he was one of the crew guys on tour, I smiled back and said hi. He proceeded to invite me into his room and told me he had some beers, if I liked that kind of thing.

I was shocked and instantly afraid. He was obviously not with our tour. I didn't know what to do and definitely didn't want him seeing which room I was staying in. If he tried anything, then my escape would be limited—I wouldn't be able to run very fast in my ankle boot.

At that moment, one of Jeremy's band members came around the corner. I was relieved and quickly signaled to him to stand with me until the creepy guy went away. But it was Jeremy who caught wind that something was wrong. Immediately, the most intimidating looked crossed Jeremy's face, and I saw him puff up in a Hulk-ish way as he asked, "What happened?"

God creates out of nothing.
Wonderful, you say. Yes
to be sure, but he does what
is still more wonderful:
he makes saints out of sinners.

SØREN KIERKEGAARD[1]

I was convinced he was going to punch this guy in the face, and I would embarrassingly be the cause of a ruckus.

I called his name to slow him down. "Jeremy!"

He didn't flinch. He strode directly toward the man and very firmly but calmly said, "Hey man, you leave our girl alone."

I think the fear of the Lord entered that guy, as it did me, and he sheepishly backed into his room.

I was entirely relieved that Jeremy had come to my defense and still nervous about being alone, so his band helped me switch rooms for the night. The next day Jeremy came and apologized for possibly scaring me. He had, but we had a good laugh about it. I was honestly thankful to have been protected.

We quickly became friends. The ice had been broken by the hotel-Hulk incident. We then had a blast being goofy, trying to out dance each other during TobyMac's set that fall. We still had no romantic interest in each other, as neither one of us thought we were each other's type, so we had an opportunity to simply enjoy our friendship. Little did we realize how foundational that friendship really was.

As the tour progressed, I heard Jeremy share briefly from the stage, and my curiosity was piqued by the reams of people lined up at his merchandise table after a show, pouring out their hearts to him—and by seeing him minister to them and comfort them in return. I watched him treat every person the same, always deeply compassionate and encouraging, no matter how many times they shared their hurts with him. Touring for him wasn't just about music; he was resolved and bold about his faith even after a heart-breaking trial that would have shaken absolutely anyone. He declared God's faithfulness unreservedly. I had never met anyone quite like him, and I was intrigued. I began asking Jeremy lots of questions about his testimony.

Neither one of us really knows when the turning point came, but I began to notice that I actually cared about where he was and what he was doing. Later on, I confessed to one of my band guys that I thought I may have had feelings for Jeremy. I wrestled with those feelings, though, because I recognized I had been in a very unhealthy place in my relationship with God, and I didn't want anything to distract me from the much-needed growth that was taking place in my heart. I had prayerfully committed to setting this season aside for just me and Jesus.

But then, Jeremy was such an anomaly. We ended up sitting next to each other often, looking for each other across the room, taking note of where the other was and what he or she was doing, and finding excuses to have conversations. It became more and more obvious how we felt about each other. I wasn't quite sure what to do with it all, so I continued to hang out with him, ask questions, and pray the Lord would take away my budding affection if it wasn't from Him.

NO GAMES ALLOWED

True to his athletic nature, especially in his younger years, Jeremy was very competitive. Once, we were with friends playing a game of pool. I'm not nearly as good as Jeremy, but it was obvious he was letting me win, and I took note of it. *Hmm...I think Jeremy likes me.* From there, our friendship rapidly evolved into something deeper. We both found any opportunity we could to interact with each other and soaked up any ounce of conversation we had with one another.

"After burying my opponent, I decided to settle for a first down." *Bruising fullback Jeremy Camp runs over a would-be tackler for a first down.*

When Jeremy and I first started dating, we spent an afternoon hanging out at a mall close to where our show was that night. He walked ahead with his friends, not paying much attention to me. I was absolutely bothered by it and decided to give him a bit of the cold shoulder. *If you won't pay attention to me, then I won't pay attention to you!* I thought.

The kinds of games you should play are Catan, Scattergories, pool, Yahtzee, Scrabble, Phase 10, Rummy, Boggle, Ticket to Ride, Cornhole, Ping-Pong, and foosball. Put down your phones, turn off the TV, laugh a lot, and make memories.

He kind of ignored it at first, but after a while he pulled me aside and asked, "What are you doing?"

I was taken aback by him acting as if he didn't know what the problem was—I was just doing what he was doing. *Two can play this game.*

He very sweetly put me in my place and told me if we were going to be together, there would be no games. He was simply walking with some friends. No harm, no foul.

Maybe I should have been put out by that, but I was instantly impressed. For him to clarify so early in our relationship that there would be no games set a standard of honesty for which I'm forever thankful.

Later, I was able to return the favor. I promised Jeremy I would never give him freedom to hang out with his friends or go do something fun if I would be silently sulking and wishing he were home with me instead. It would be unfair of me to tell him, "I'm fine; you can go," when I'm not fine and secretly resent him.

So we made a deal: Don't say you're okay when you're not. Keep it simple and uncomplicated.

— Jeremy's Journal —

One of the best things I learned during this season of basically courting Adrienne was the importance of laying all my cards on the table. In the beginning stages of getting to know someone, most people like to put their best foot forward. But because of what I had walked through before I met Adrienne, I was going to do nothing of the sort. Questions were asked, hypothetical scenarios were brought up. We discussed basically anything so we could *really* get to know each other.

That may sound a bit aggressive or perhaps too regimented to some, but committing to honesty definitely gave us a crash course in understanding what made the other tick. I don't regret that. It is better to learn about each other before you dive into a marriage with unknowns looming than to find out the truth about your spouse when it's too late.

That doesn't mean that when you get married you've learned everything there is to know about the other person; there are things you don't even realize about yourself until you are living day to day with someone else. Part of the beauty of marriage is learning the ins and outs and good and bad of the one you love and walking through it with them.

— Adrienne's Journal —

I never felt unsafe with Jeremy. I knew he said what he meant, and he wasn't stringing me along. We were building our friendship for a reason. Our intentions for a long-term relationship had been made clear, and I could trust him to keep his word even though we weren't engaged yet. His honesty showed me his maturity and the strength of his character.

Relationship games only hurt—and there is never a winner. Back up your words with actions. Build a lasting friendship and talk through as much as possible before you get married.

Long-distance relationships aren't necessarily a bad thing. When our touring schedules differed, we had nothing but conversation as an option for spending time together. Oftentimes we talked until we fell asleep—sometimes until 3:00 or 4:00 in the morning!

APPLEBEE'S "PROPOSAL"

One day Jeremy invited me out for dinner. But contrary to what you may be thinking, I had a sense he was going to shut down our whole relationship. I even told a friend that I thought he would break it off with me. Although we hadn't fully defined our relationship yet, we both knew we were more than friends. I was bummed at the thought of that changing, but I didn't know for sure what would happen, so I just waited until the evening to see what he was thinking.

Although I was enjoying hanging out with Adrienne, I constantly felt guilty about having feelings for her. It had been a hard season getting used to life without my first wife, Melissa, and the thought of entrusting my heart to someone else again left me feeling extremely vulnerable. But something drew me to Adrienne and kept me wanting to build a friendship with her. I knew I would have to decide whether or not I was going to continue pursuing her and make our relationship serious and permanent. In that moment, I was leaning toward taking a huge step back.

I took Adrienne to a restaurant close to that night's venue. Unfortunately there wasn't much to choose from—too cheap would be disrespectful, but too nice and she might get her hopes up—so Applebee's would have to be the one. We sat down and ordered our food, sensing some kind of tension as we floundered through conversation. All of a sudden I blurted out, "Do you think you could marry me?"

Without hesitation, she opened her mouth and said, "Yes!"

I couldn't believe she responded so quickly, and I couldn't believe that's what I had asked her.

There was a moment of stunned silence, and we stared at each other awkwardly while nervously picking at our food. I told her I'd had every intention of breaking things off with her that night, but when it came time to follow through with it, I couldn't bring myself to say the words.

She told me she had sensed that was the case, but she was glad I chose not to follow through.

Neither one of us were really sure what had just happened. We hardly ate anything. Filled with nervous excitement and so many thoughts rolling around in our heads, we headed back to the tour buses hand in hand. We knew we weren't officially engaged, but our conversation had most definitely set the tone for our relationship. We were committed to building something with the intention of marriage.

We were protective of our tender new friendship. It was immensely precious to us—like nothing either of us had ever experienced—and we didn't want anyone to mess with it or anything to disturb it. It was a relief not to have the emotional game playing so many people experience in their relationships.

We began praying for each other often and started reading the same passages of Scripture so we could talk about what the Lord was showing us each day. Our friendship deepened. We didn't know when or how our relationship would unfold; this was just the beginning.

I still battled with guilt from time to time, but the Lord spoke to my heart one day and said, "If I'm giving you a blessing, you can receive it with joy." And Adrienne felt she needed the approval of my family and all my friends who had faithfully walked the hardest of roads with me. Our situation was very delicate in many ways, but we knew it was the beginning of a deeply special friendship, and we were so excited about what God had for us together.

I know the plans I have for you, declares the LORD, plans for welfare and not for evil, to give you a future and a hope. Then you will call upon me and come and pray to me, and I will hear you. You will seek me and find me, when you seek me with all your heart.

JEREMIAH 29:11-13

Contract vs. Covenant

There is a big difference between a contract and a covenant, as this partial list from *UpCounsel* shows:

- *While a contract is legally binding, a covenant is a spiritual agreement.*
- *You seal a covenant while you sign a contract.*
- *A contract exchanges one good for another, while a covenant is giving oneself to the other.*
- *You can opt out of a contract, while a covenant is about having the strength to hold up your part of the promise.*[2]

Today, one of the most common types of covenant might be the neighborhood covenant. When you buy a home, especially in a planned, suburban neighborhood, you are sometimes asked to sign a "covenant" that commits you to paying certain fees, maintaining your property to a set standard, and maybe even behaving in a certain way. It doesn't matter whether or not your neighbors are following the covenant—you are bound to fulfill your promise to the community. Your dues must be paid, your lawn must be mowed, and your music can't be too loud.

Covenants were much more common and meaningful in the ancient world. The first thorough description of one in the Bible comes in Genesis 15:7-21. God asks Abram to butcher several animals and lay the halves on the ground in two columns: each animal's left side on the left, and each animal's right side on the right. Between them was an open path.

Under normal circumstances, when two men were involved in making a covenant (instead of one man and God), both participants would walk down the path, symbolically saying to the other, "If I break this covenant, then may this type of death be done to me." In Abram's case, only God committed Himself to the covenant; only God passed between the carcasses. He promised that Abram would have many descendants from his biological offspring, and that those descendants would rule the area.

Even before God made a covenant with Abram, He knew He would faithfully covenant Himself to an unfaithful people. No matter how many times they failed to follow Him—and the Old Testament is filled with stories of just that—He always made a way for restoration in their relationship.

In the New Testament, God's relationship with us is described as a way-less-gruesome kind of covenant: a marriage covenant. God loves and pursues His church, the bride, based on who He is and not based on our faithfulness, for we know we have fallen far short (Romans 3:23). God the Father loved us first and sealed us with the promise of His Spirit, through the death and resurrection of His Son, Jesus.

He is a covenantal God, not contractual. We do not earn His unending love; He has given it to us freely and unreservedly, even though we did not choose Him. There are so many people who know the Holy Spirit was wooing them even before they committed to following Him. He is ever patient and never gives up on us. Jesus has an unquenchable love for His church, an unyielding, never-ending fire in His heart for her. He pursues her passionately and fiercely.

God's covenanted love is outside of time. It transcends boundaries, cultures, hurts, dysfunctions, pain, scars, and the deepest wounds. This is also the type of supernatural love offered to each of us for our marriages. When we get married, yes, we sign a legally binding contract, but we also make a beautiful covenant with each other before God. As husband and wife become one, each promises to remain committed to the other regardless of the other's willingness to pay dues, mow the lawn, or turn down the music. Such unconditional love is not possible in human hearts, so God—who has never broken a covenant—is the best one to hold the couple together.

God is not man, that he should lie, or a
son of man, that he should change his mind.
Has he said, and will he not do it?
Or has he spoken, and will he not
fulfill it?

NUMBERS 23:19

Know therefore that the LORD your God is
God, the faithful God who keeps covenant
and steadfast love with those who love
him and keep his commandments, to a
thousand generations.

DEUTERONOMY 7:9

A WEDDING STORY

Adrienne planned our wedding while living out of a little vintage green suitcase in The Benjamin Gate's white 15-passenger van as they traveled around the country. When she finished up her season touring with the band, she moved to Indiana to live with my family for three months, where she continued to plan the wedding from an old table in my parents' basement. She made all the invitations and created all the decorations. Needless to say, there was glitter and glue stuck to every nook and cranny of the room.

The Invitations

The plan was for us to be married in Port Elizabeth, South Africa, in hot sunny December, but due to complications regarding Adrienne's visa just three months before the actual wedding, we had to hastily change plans to a winter wedding in Lafayette, Indiana. It was the Christmas season, so the only available date was Monday, December 15, 2003—right smack-dab in the middle

The Addresses

of a cold winter. It snowed the morning of our ceremony, covering the ground with a white, soft dusting.

Despite the oddities and hiccups, the details of our small wedding came together beautifully. A few of Adrienne's close friends from South Africa were able to make it to the States, and I was finally able to meet her family three days before we were married. It's a good thing they liked me! Can you imagine how awkward that would have been if they hadn't?

Meet the Parents

The Lord gave Adrienne a scripture for the wedding:

They will enter Zion with singing;
everlasting joy will crown their heads.
Gladness and joy will overtake them,
and sorrow and sighing will flee away.

ISAIAH 51:11 NIV

— Adrienne's Journal —

Some people tell you to "date around" so you can figure out what you want in a partner. I entirely disagree. The more people you date, the messier things get. There is *zero* part of me on this side of "I do" that wishes I had kissed more boys or had more relationships.

Don't believe the lies of the world for a second. When you find "the one" who is more special to you than anyone you've ever met, you realize what a deep treasure every part of your relationship is, and you don't want anyone but your best friend to have all of you. There's no way you would wish you had more interactions and memories with other people—what good would those be? You would just end up with pieces of your heart scattered everywhere, baggage you have to carry around with you, and a world of insecurities to sort through.

You're building *your* story, not some unrealistic romantic drama. You don't need to find out whether you're physically compatible (that's a no-brainer and the world's way of thinking!); you have your whole marriage to grow in this area. The best and most lasting way to grow together is to follow God's plan for your relationship. In doing this, you will find the sweetest and greatest rewards. Why would you want to spoil the lifelong adventure you can have with your spouse as you learn about each other and grow old together? That is the best kind of love story!

I charge you:
Do not arouse or awaken love
until it so desires.

SONG OF SONGS 8:4 NIV

2

CULTURE SHOCK

After a few years of marriage, I noticed Jeremy had a habit of pacing around the house when he returned home from being on the road. It was almost as if he had to refamiliarize himself with his surroundings as his way of decompressing. He wasn't picky, but there were definitely certain things he liked to have in their place. For instance, he would be overwhelmed by toys lying around, but he couldn't care less if there were dishes in the sink.

Since I was juggling two littles at the time, I would spend hours cleaning and vacuuming, only to have the house unraveled within minutes. These artistic little creatures had a way of tornado-ing through the house like none other.

One time I decided to follow Jeremy through the house to notice what he was looking at when he arrived home. Instead of stressing out about cleaning the entire house every time he came home, I started to focus on the main spots he noticed and organize or clean those first. The new routine was effective for both of us.

There was so much for us to figure out about each other after we got married. For instance, I grew up with a family who loved to debate their opinions, especially on sports and politics. My dad and his brothers would argue and then high-five and hug one another afterward. The adults were free to express themselves, even in disagreement. Debate was like a rite of passage.

Jeremy's parents hardly ever argued, and if they did, it was behind closed doors and quietly—so he certainly wasn't expecting us to have moments of severe clashing. If we argued or disagreed on something, especially with any amount of passion, he felt disrespected or thought perhaps we had some serious relational issues.

We had to learn that both of our families had valid ways of looking at and working through issues. Neither option was better than the other, and we had to decide the rules for our own disagreements in order to fight well together.

LEARNING ABOUT EACH OTHER

With Jeremy being a touring musician, his travel schedule demands we be away from each other often. After our first child, Isabella, was born, Jeremy hit the road for a month. It was so hard. I was alone with our new baby girl, and he was heartbroken to be away from us. After that month apart, we decided never to spend more than two weeks away from each other unless it was absolutely out of our control. In 16 years, we have kept this commitment, with only a few exceptions when either of us has had to travel internationally.

After a while, our two girls and I had a solid routine. I could change diapers with lightning speed, juggle two babies, get dinner ready, grab all the groceries, and rock whatever cleaning needed to be done. I was swimming along in every aspect of motherhood, mostly alone. When Jeremy came home, he would interrupt our groove a little. But I am so thankful for the Holy Spirit's leading, because very quickly the Lord showed me to give Jeremy space to figure out parenting as well.

I learned to step back and give him room to lead and be who he is to the kids, because God had given my children both a mom and a dad for a reason. There were definitely times I had to make a conscious decision to let him do things his way, even if I had already figured out a shortcut. No matter how much faster or even better I could handle the toddlers, they also needed him. They needed his perspective and personality, and he had so much he could contribute to our family, even if he handled situations in a way I wouldn't have handled them.

As I stepped back, Jeremy noticed things about both of our girls that had escaped me. God gave him revelation into each of them that I had

completely missed. Sometimes our culture paints fathers as emotionally clueless, but I can assure you that it has often been the insights of Jeremy and even my own dad that have brought necessary wisdom and direction.

Fathers, don't underestimate your role and ability to

lead and speak into the lives of your children. Your strength, oversight, and voice are very much needed, even when your children are grown.

THE FAILED GETAWAY

Before Jeremy and I got married, my precious dad took me out for lunch to give me some marriage advice, which included a little pep talk about giving guys space. He talked about how sometimes they just need to retreat into a "cave" and have time to process. Of course, I thought he clearly didn't know Jeremy very well and must have been talking about every other guy except for him because Jeremy was unlike anyone I had ever met.

However, early in our marriage, I found myself learning that very lesson. As soon as there was any type of conflict between us, I wanted to hash it out and talk it through right then and there—to "beat this thing," you know? So I would push and push to figure it all out. I couldn't leave it alone, not for a second. When Jeremy wasn't as equally ready to talk, it felt like he was giving up. Or perhaps I saw Jeremy's withdrawal as rejection and couldn't handle it.

On one occasion, he was desperate to walk out, and I had the ingenious idea of using my body as a human barricade in the doorway, doing whatever I could to stop my extremely aggravated husband from leaving. I'm pretty sure he just needed space to mull over everything I had already verbally thrown at him, but I didn't see it that way, and I just wouldn't stop pushing the issue. Anyway, Jeremy and I do not physically compare. He simply picked me up by my shoulders, lifted me off my feet, and placed me out of the way.

As he rushed toward the garage to go for a drive, I tried to outwit him and confiscated his car keys. Our pulses running hot and both of us fuming, he juked and grabbed my keys, so I beelined for the front seat of the car with his keys still in hand, all the while thinking, *Ha! I've got you now. You cannot leave, and you will talk this out with me!*

(I mean, how stupid can we be in arguments—as if this sort of scene would bring about a relationship-deepening discussion!)

He was so mad that he bolted out of the car and took off pacing down the street. It was late on a January night and around 30 degrees outside. He was dressed in sweatpants, a T-shirt, and flip-flops.

After unsuccessfully trying to prevent his departure, I had enough sense not to follow him down the road and leave our two sleeping babies behind. I watched him walk away.

At first, I felt victorious for having stopped his attempt to drive off and leave me, but when I went inside the house and closed the door, I instantly felt regret for how I had behaved. I had gone way too far. No kidding. I got on my knees and started praying. I confessed my ridiculousness to the Lord and prayed for Him to soften Jeremy's heart toward me.

Unbeknownst to me, Jeremy was absolutely freezing after walking a few miles without the appropriate outerwear. He also started to realize his plan of checking himself into a hotel for the night—without his wife—wouldn't look so good in the small community in which we lived. A little while later, my phone rang: "Hey, babe, can you come pick me up?"

To which I gushed, "Oh my darling, I'm so sorry—yes! I'll be right there."

In those early days of our marriage, we quickly realized we had the capacity to pull either the best out of each other or the worst. Marriage is unique. As you grow in your friendship and love, you realize how vulnerable you are

I doubt God keeps track of how many arguments we win; God may indeed keep track of how well we love.

PHILIP YANCEY[1]

to each other. *You see all of me—physically, emotionally, spiritually. Will you still love me? Will you still cheer me on?* We see each other's worst, but if we stick around, we also get to see the best.

Jeremy and I are still working on this, but we have learned to give each other space and time to process. By no means does that mean sweeping disagreements under the rug and forgetting about them. Nope, not at all.

Deal with your issues. Talk about them. But be fully aware that timing for good conversations (that is, *productive* conversations) is key. Allow each other room to calm down, and while you're waiting, pray. Pray for each other, inviting Jesus into the middle of it all. Perhaps you think that's a tad extreme, especially when both of you are fired up or screaming at each other, but try it anyway. Jesus is watching it all, and I'm pretty sure He would rather be in the middle of it, giving you supernatural love and forgiveness, than see you continue to tear each other apart.

One thing that forced us to give each other time to process was being away from each other on the road. There were times when we were in the middle of an argument or a tense situation, and Jeremy would have to go play a show, do an interview, or address something else that demanded his immediate attention. This ended up being very good for us early on because it gave those situations time to simmer down.

How many of us end up relinquishing silly arguments if just given a bit of time to breathe? An hour goes by, and all of a sudden we can see the pettiness in some of our thinking. Or perhaps as we pour out our frustrations to the Lord, He gives us His perspective on the issue.

Try arguing with someone who is walking in humility. Try arguing with someone who is quickly willing to own their wrongs. The argument doesn't go very far.

Have you ever thought about what Jesus thinks conflict should look like? If we note how He acted while on earth, we'll see that He confronted people in their sin, pushed back on their ideas, challenged the cultural norm, and spoke truth with boldness, yet in love and respect. Ultimately, when He challenged someone or brought something to the table, it was for the hearer's growth so they could take a step closer to understanding God.

How often do we fight selfishly? We fight to have our perspectives seen or to get our points across. "Love me, understand me, give in to me and what I want, see my side, pay more attention to me…"

James 4:1-2 says, "Where do you think all these appalling wars and quarrels come from? Do you think they just happen? Think again. They come about because you want your own way, and fight for it deep inside yourselves. You lust for what you don't have and are willing to kill to get it" (MSG). I'm sure Jeremy and I are not the only ones whose bad arguments reek of selfishness and pride. But try arguing with someone who is walking in humility. Try arguing with someone who is quickly willing to own their wrongs. The argument doesn't go very far.

Don't repay evil for evil.
Don't retaliate with insults
when people insult you.
Instead, pay them back with
a blessing. That is what God
has called you to do, and he
will grant you his blessing.

1 PETER 3:9 NLT

Summing up: Be agreeable,
be sympathetic, be loving, be
compassionate, be humble. That
goes for all of you, no exceptions.
No retaliation. No sharp-tongued
sarcasm. Instead, bless—that's your
job, to bless. You'll be a blessing
and also get a blessing.

1 PETER 3:8-9 MSG

CONFLICT...UGH!

When you first meet that special someone, you don't think much about what your arguments will be like. You think about how wonderful they make you feel and how awesome they are. But as much as you might quiz each other about how many kids you want to have together, your genetic dispositions, where you want to live, your life goals, etc., you might want to add to your list, "How do we plan on fighting?"

Too many people try to avoid conflict altogether, but the sooner the two of you realize that it's unavoidable, the better it will be for your friendship. There is absolutely no way you can build a relationship without having conflict, so start thinking about how to fight well.

Set parameters before a fight starts—and revisit them from time to time. Update them and tweak them, but agree on what is acceptable arguing. It is vital to talk through these things before you're wanting to gouge each other's eyes out:

Is it okay to disagree? How do we do this respectfully? Is it okay to be snarky to each other in public? Is it okay to yell? How do we avoid pushing each other's "crazy" buttons? How do we feel about walking out in the middle of a conversation or ignoring each other? If we need space, how can we communicate that in honor? How far do we push? Can we recognize when a situation is going nowhere fast and agree to talk at a later time? Is sarcasm allowed? How about name calling? Can we agree that these hard discussions need to grow us as a team?

A good question to ask yourself is, *Would I mind if this were done to me?* Put yourself in the other's shoes. How would you want to be treated?

Remember, you are fighting alongside each other, against the enemy of your souls and your marriage. Your spouse is not the enemy. I repeat: Your spouse is *not* the enemy. What good can come from a conversation about

> My beloved brothers, understand this:
> Everyone should be quick to listen,
> slow to speak, and slow to anger, for
> man's anger does not bring about
> the righteousness that God desires.
> Therefore, get rid of all moral filth and
> every expression of evil, and humbly
> receive the word planted in you, which
> can save your souls.
>
> JAMES 1:19-21 BSB

how annoying your spouse is, or how much you think you have to put up with? Is there a better way to communicate what's on your heart? Are you building up your marriage or tearing it down?

Act wisely. Protect yourself from misunderstandings when you're tired. Don't presume to know how someone is processing a scenario; rather, ask. If we react based on presumption and are wrong, then we end up causing a scene for no good reason.

One of my favorite marriage books is called *Fight Fair!*[2] In it, the authors wrote about praying together in the middle of an argument. I laughed out loud when I read that because, in the past, my arguments with Jeremy were far from a time of sacred prayer together. We had had those soul-watering times, but not usually in the middle of an argument. Instead, there were generally attacks, defenses, rebuttals, verbal jabs and blocks—you get the message. Not pretty.

Instead of continuing to make defenses for myself, I started asking the Lord to help me communicate the issues on my heart, change me where I am wrong, and help me forgive without bitterness or resentment. I asked the Holy Spirit to help us find a way to hear and understand each other. When my pride was reeling and refusing to relent, I asked the Lord to help me *feel* sorry and to hear what Jeremy had to say, even if I didn't think he was worthy to listen to in the heat of the moment.

Your spouse is not evil. Instead of thinking, *What in the world got into them?* ask yourself, *What are they trying to communicate through this conflict?* Find a healing middle ground, remember who the real enemy is, and remember who is on your side. "If God is for us, who can be against us?" (Romans 8:31).

Which One Are You?

Over the years there have been various fads in personality tests. When I was in high school, we tested to see whether we were sanguine, choleric, phlegmatic, or melancholic. There was another test where we'd be described as an animal—lion, otter, golden retriever, or beaver. It's probably because of my personality type, but I couldn't understand how psychologists managed to assign the complex human soul to one of four categories. This classification bothered me immensely, especially when I had a characteristic or two from every chart. *Oh no! Which one am I? This could lead to greater problems. How can I answer these questions to fall into the column I want to be in?*

Jeremy once had a radio interview where they asked him which categories we fell into. He told them he was the lion and I was the beaver. They proceeded to announce over the air that we were the worst combination. It's a good thing we weren't looking to personality tests for our marital direction when we first met, or else we would have missed the best adventure of our lives. Since then, I'm relieved to say psychologists have come up with more comprehensive personality tests.

A couple years ago we were going through a stage in our marriage where we were clashing quite a bit. It felt like no matter how hard we tried, we just couldn't understand where the other person was coming from. Coincidentally we took two different personality tests around the same time.

We were just doing it for fun and had no idea how much the results would impact our understanding of each other.

We started seeing things in light of whom God had created each of us to be. Instead of feeling or thinking that Jeremy was just downright crazy or that I had quirks he just couldn't wrap his head around, we had fresh insight into each other's heart and wiring.

The tests also helped us see how other people might view our strengths and weaknesses. We all tend to give ourselves plenty of slack because we know where we are coming from or what our hearts' intentions are in the moment. We often give ourselves the benefit of the doubt, but stepping back and seeing our personalities from someone else's perspective is vital to building a good friendship.

We need to have tenderness and patience for each other's weaknesses or places of immaturity (as my dad calls them, "young places"). We all have them. We've all had difficult situations in life that have scarred us with different levels of undesired brokenness or dysfunction, and we are all inherently wired to look out for ourselves. But as we engage with the Lord, we have the rest of our lives to let Him change us to be like Him and to perfect His love in us. The sooner we realize that marriage is a journey, the better. You do not arrive at perfection the day you get married. This is a commitment to becoming best friends and traveling through the rest of life together.

Two are better than one,

because they have a good return for their labor:

If either of them falls down,

one can help the other up.

But pity anyone who falls

and has no one to help them up.

Also, if two lie down together, they will keep warm.

But how can one keep warm alone?

Though one may be overpowered,

two can defend themselves.

A cord of three strands is not quickly broken.

ECCLESIASTES 4:9-12 NIV

What are some things you can implement in your marriage to find out more about the way you're both wired and what makes your spouse tick? Remember, what we put into our marriage is what we'll get out.

Advice from Jeremy

Dealing with conflict and building great communication practices are essential to a growing friendship and marriage. Avoiding the hard issues doesn't make them go away, but it will make your relationship shallow and unfruitful. Your problems will remain until you address them. You may be cordial with each other, but there can be no real connection.

Instill habits to build your level of communication and be willing to change. If you accuse your spouse by saying, "You always..." or, "You never..." then they have to defend themselves. Believe the best first. Be willing to hear, and don't just push your own agenda to be heard.

Adrienne once asked, "If I promise to keep quiet and not say a word, would you tell me what you're thinking? I want to know your heart. What is the deeper issue?" She promised to listen and not interrupt me, which made me less defensive, and we were able to resolve the issue that had been bothering us both. It was an effective strategy because her willing silence gave me the freedom to talk openly. It's so important to give each other a place to be heard.

Prayer

Lord Jesus, we are desperate for You. We need You to do the impossible for us. Help us walk with each other in humility when life seems out of control. Help us honor each other and not be focused on our own selfish needs. Help us remember to bring You into the center of everything—yes, even our arguments. By Your grace and Your strength alone can we do these things. Amen.

How much room do we give each other to learn, to make mistakes and grow?

Get rid of all bitterness, rage, anger, harsh words, and slander, as well as all types of evil behavior. Instead, be kind to each other, tenderhearted, forgiving one another, just as God through Christ has forgiven you.

EPHESIANS 4:31-32 NLT

3

THE BACK BURNER

A few years into our marriage, my career exploded, and its demands and pressures increased dramatically. All of a sudden, when I went out in public, strangers would approach me for photos or conversation. They were always kind and encouraging, but I'd never before experienced such publicity.

Adrienne and I both felt we were being watched more than usual.

I remember a time when we had gone days without seeing each other. Adrienne had driven four hours to the location of one of my shows with our daughter Bella, who was about five months old at the time. We were desperate for some family time and only had the morning alone together before Adrienne had to drive back and I had to keep going with the tour. We went out to eat for breakfast, and as we were trying to enjoy the inadequate few hours we had together, we were interrupted by two different people wanting photos. Of course they meant no harm, but Adrienne was irritated and distinctly remembers having to prayerfully ask the Lord to help her lay the privacy of our family at His feet. We were learning the cost of ministry in the public eye.

The travel was intense. I was playing anywhere from 150 to 200 shows a year, in addition to writing and recording albums (11 in 17 years), doing radio and magazine interviews, participating in photo and video shoots, and numerous other publicity opportunities that come with the territory. Adrienne led worship at our church, was involved in women's ministry, and released two solo albums. Plus, she and the girls would travel with me as often as possible.

Needless to say, our family very quickly learned to be flexible with every changing scenario. I'm sure it

was hilarious to watch us unpack the car like a Mary Poppins bag—pulling out car seats, strollers, cribs, foldable high chairs, toys, diapers—and haul it all onto the bus, where the kids took baths in the tiny kitchen sink. Taking kids on planes, trains, and automobiles is no easy feat with a tantrum here and there, dirty diapers, projectile vomiting, and food allergies, to name a few challenges. For the sake of survival, Adrienne and I would remind each other that every travel experience was an adventure—like a jack-in-the-box, we weren't quite sure when something would pop up on each trip.

All these challenges were setting us up for incredible life experiences. But juggling overflowing schedules and two beautiful baby girls—only 18 months apart—took its toll. As they say, "If you have too much on your plate, something will inevitably fall off."

I would often come home so exhausted from traveling and constantly pouring

Bella in the bus's sink

myself out that the little I had left to give would go toward the girls. Lasting scars from watching my first wife suffer still cut deep into my heart. Although I never felt the Lord would allow something to happen to Adrienne, I struggled to trust that something wouldn't happen to our girls. The result was fear and anxiety. There were times I would spiral downward from the stress of the industry, the expectations people put on me, and the pressure I put on myself to be a good father and husband. It felt suffocating.

Adrienne was just as exhausted from juggling life—oftentimes as a single mom—and always having to pour herself out as she raised the girls without my constant presence. One day I came home and our oldest, Bella, wouldn't talk to me for three days. She completely ignored me. We were devastated. It was then I realized that the children didn't have the ability to comprehend my comings and goings.

Adrienne started doing different creative countdowns to help the girls anticipate when I would come home, and I started taking them out on intentional daddy-daughter dates before I would leave again. We realized quality was more important than quantity, which has since become foundational for us. I could be home every day and still never build a relationship with my kids or wife. The important thing is

to take time to be present with them, to get to know them and pour into them, and to build and establish our relationships.

In that season, we were struggling to maneuver around so many different dynamics and demands. I was battling fear and control. Adrienne felt like she was on my back burner—just getting my emotional leftovers—which, in actuality, she was.

You have the greatest capacity to hurt the person you're closest to. There is a unique vulnerability you experience in marriage because you have given all of who you are to each other. Adrienne and I were (and still are) learning each other's wiring; we realized we could push buttons no one else could.

With the vulnerability comes fragility, as well as power to truly build up or tear down. We had arguments in which we pushed each other to the limit—and afterward, with broken hearts, realized that was not the way we wanted to treat each other, nor was it what we wanted our marriage to be. We wanted to outlast all the heartache life threw at us, and we had to learn, on a much deeper level, how to tap into supernatural love to build an unshakable foundation of friendship that can only be found in Jesus. We had to learn to walk in grace, patience, and forgiveness, gleaning wisdom and guidance from the Scriptures—and, of course, through much prayer.

Umbrella of Mercy

Marriage is a blast. You get to learn all sorts of interesting things about each other, including the funny quirks and idiosyncrasies we all have. Perhaps you just thought everyone else was weird, but now you have to come to grips with the thought that you might be weird too.

One of those peculiarities I had to learn about Jeremy was his extremism. He is a grab-the-bull-by-the-horns kind of guy. He will dive into a situation headfirst without hesitation. He is constantly dreaming of new ideas and ventures. I, on the other hand, am fairly reserved. I like factors that make sense, and I have to analyze them before I commit to an idea. Once I'm in, I'm all in, but I'm a bit of a skeptic initially.

At the beginning of our marriage, I would have mini, internal panic attacks every time Jeremy would expound on his wild ideas, but after some time I understood that I didn't have to say much, because most of the time he was simply thinking out loud. He was having fun dreaming and planning, even if the ideas didn't come to fruition.

A close friend told us about a concept called "the umbrella of mercy." It simply means providing a safe place to openly discuss ideas and dreams without holding someone accountable or expecting the plans to come to fruition. It has been wonderful for us. It freed Jeremy to talk and dream without restraint, and it freed me from worrying he was going to pursue everything he was thinking about!

Not Our Thing

Neither one of us is super big on celebrating gift-industry-appropriated holidays such as Valentine's Day. It means far more to me, personally, for Jeremy to be spontaneous—to send me flowers or buy me something thoughtful on any other day of the year than on days our culture has pre-determined. On many special occasions, because of his travel schedule, we cannot be together. We may be away on birthdays, anniversaries, and occasions like those, but we'll make it up some other time.

Newlyweds, December 2003

Very early on, we decided flexibility is key: It's not a matter of when we celebrate, but that we do celebrate. When we got married, my parents flew all the way from South Africa and met Jeremy for the first time three days before the wedding. So instead of going away on a honeymoon, we only went away for a couple days and came home early to spend time with family. We have joked that skipping our honeymoon gave us license for all the fun trips we've taken since then.

Now, this may be the complete opposite of what works for you and your significant other; these special days may be very much a part of your dynamic. There is nothing wrong with that. Don't compare your own groove to what other people are doing. Sow life into your friendship, however you end up building it.

HOW MANY PRAYERS?

Are you asking God to change your spouse instead of your heart? Are you asking Him to take action on your loved one's sin while ignoring the role you play in it? When you pray for your spouse in times of conflict or stretching, are you praying with wrong motives? Perhaps you have unrealistic expectations that the world says should be filled. It's imperative to ask, "God, what are You showing *me*?"

> What is causing the quarrels and fights among you? Don't they come from the evil desires at war within you? You want what you don't have, so you scheme and kill to get it. You are jealous of what others have, but you can't get it, so you fight and wage war to take it away from them. Yet you don't have what you want because you don't ask God for it. And even when you ask, you don't get it because your motives are all wrong—you want only what will give you pleasure…
>
> So humble yourselves before God. Resist the devil, and he will flee from you. Come close to God, and God will come close to you. Wash your hands, you sinners; purify your hearts, for your loyalty is divided between God and the world. Let there be tears for what you have done. Let there be sorrow and deep grief. Let there be sadness instead of laughter, and gloom instead of joy. Humble yourselves before the Lord, and he will lift you up in honor (James 4:1-3,7-10 NLT).

Have you tried praying for a new and fresh love? Pray God will give you eyes to see your loved one the way He sees them. Ask Him to fill you anew with love and forgiveness like you've never had before—or with the respect you desperately need. You may have reached a point in your relationship where you're having a hard time seeing anything good in each other, but the Father's love never runs dry. He is an endless source of endurance and hope for every shortcoming you will ever see or have,

and He will never stop loving you. He has grace for the rubs that have come and the ones that will.

We have been in this place where we both needed to cry out to the Lord and ask Him to soften our hearts for each other. As we have asked, the Lord has answered faithfully.

It is not so true that "prayer changes things" as that prayer changes me and I change things. God has so constituted things that prayer on the basis of Redemption alters the way in which a man looks at things. Prayer is not a question of altering things externally, but of working wonders in a man's disposition.

OSWALD CHAMBERS[1]

I heard a story about a girl whose family was experiencing serious difficulties. Her father prayed and asked God for help that he felt must be given—and must be given soon. She noticed a sign on the wall of her parents' bedroom with the motto "Prayer changes things." As she heard her father praying with increasing intensity, she looked at the motto and wondered, *Does prayer really change things?*

The trouble they were facing developed into a definite crisis, and her father's prayers were not answered in the way for which he had asked. He said nothing, but the next morning, after God had given the answer in a different way, the daughter noticed a black line had been drawn through the word *things* on the sign. Above it, her father had printed the word *me*. It now read, "Prayer changes me."

How many times do we get frustrated with God because He doesn't answer the way we think He ought to answer? Sometimes I wonder, *Who do*

To you they cried and were rescued; in you they trusted and were not put to shame.

PSALM 22:5

we think we are anyway? Our Father is "in heaven" (Matthew 6:9). Do we remember our position? We are dust, and we have been given free access to commune with the magnificent Creator of the universe, who has unending love for us. I'm sure He has the capacity to hold our world together without hearing our instructions.

We need to rightly align ourselves with Him. Maybe He isn't answering our prayers because *we* need changing, not our circumstances.

We've often talked to our kids about how prayer isn't just dumping everything you want on Jesus and then signing out. He's not our "drive-through Jesus"—we can't put in our orders, get a quick fix of junk food, and then drive off. Prayer is meant to change us. It's meant to nourish our souls. It's meant for us to commune with the Lord so He can leave His divine imprint on us.

There may be times when your circumstances change through prayer, but not always. When you find yourself wondering why your surroundings are the same after much prayer, ask if the Lord needs to do some deeper refinement of your heart.

This may seem like an unreliable, scary place for some who don't know that the Father's heart for us is good. He doesn't withhold gifts from us because He is stingy, especially if those good gifts have the ability to make us more like Jesus. Oftentimes, there are areas of our flesh that need to be starved. This starvation of our flesh isn't just about the death itself, but about the life that emerges after we have relinquished everything. If Jesus had never defeated death by His resurrection, we wouldn't have the hope and power of the gospel message; He would simply have been a phenomenal

Now if any of you lacks wisdom, he should ask God, who gives generously to all without finding fault, and it will be given to him. But he must ask in faith, without doubting, because he who doubts is like a wave of the sea, blown and tossed by the wind. That man should not expect to receive anything from the Lord. He is a double-minded man, unstable in all his ways.

JAMES 1:5-8 BSB

man. Our lives need to reflect the resurrection power, which is essentially the crux of the gospel.

It may be hard to imagine what it looks like for our marriages to be filled with resurrected power and supernatural love found in the nature of Jesus when we have little to no love left for each other. But through prayer, God can fill our hearts—so hardened by unforgiveness or hurt—with overflowing affection and desire. He breathes healing life into us, our walls come down, and the hardness melts away, giving us the grace to walk through difficult times together. Now we see why the need of Him should be what binds and weaves us together. We walk in the supernatural abilities of Jesus.

Jesus is the king of taking your scraps—five loaves and two fish (see Matthew 14:17-20)—and doing something supernatural with whatever you bring Him. Don't scoff at what you're holding out to Him; just bring it all. Be amazed at His character. There is no other God like Him. He really does receive the offerings of your broken things and then turn them into something beautiful. Of course, He is worthy of more than just your brokenness, but He will never turn you away.

MAKE TIME

During our dating days, we were living in different states (Adrienne was in Tennessee while I was in California) and both touring full-time, so most of our relationship was long distance as we zigzagged all over the country. In order to be intentional about making Jesus the center of our friendship, we chose to read the same section of Scripture together and talk about what stood out to us. This commitment wasn't obligatory or legalistic—we loved it. It was so much fun sharing the different things God was showing each of us in Scripture, and we found the other's insight refreshing and encouraging.

We were honestly thankful for the initial distance because the only thing we could do was talk. And we would talk for hours on end. Once, when Adrienne was visiting her family in South Africa, our phone bill was more than $1,000 for the month (and that was more than 17 years ago). Yikes! Young love!

We have continued this pattern of pursuing Jesus together in different ways. We have family nights with a time of worship and prayer, sometimes going through a devotional together. We value sitting down at the dinner table and sharing a meal. Our kids love when we ask, "High and low?" and we all get to share what our high and low moments of the week were. Although we don't ever have a set schedule in our family, because travel days and tours will vary at different times of the year, we always make an effort to connect. It's vitally important to seek Jesus together and not have Him be just a piece of our pie. He is the One who weaves together our love and renews us every day. There is no way we could flourish in this life without Him.

A Daily Prayer Guide for Couples

Holy Spirit, help us grow in these ways:

- May we be humble people of prayer, maturing in the Lord, ever growing in our knowledge of You (2 Peter 3:18) so that we may be found complete in You (2 Timothy 3:16-17).

- May we act as purely in private as we profess to do publicly, and may we be able to relax and unwind (physically, mentally, emotionally) without sinning against You.

- May we learn to "take every thought captive" (2 Corinthians 10:5) and not to be conformed to the world's thinking, but to renew our minds and think scripturally and obediently (Romans 12:2).

- May we learn not to depend upon our circumstances, each other, or things for happiness and fulfillment, but on You alone (Habakkuk 3:17-19).

- May we rejoice in You and have no confidence in who we are or what we have done (Philippians 3:3,8-9).

- May our sense of significance and self-image be a reflection of Your thoughts toward us (Psalm 139).

- May we have new, increased strength (Isaiah 40:31) and be "rooted and grounded in love" in the middle of life's circumstances (Ephesians 3:17; see also Philippians 4:12-13).

- May the fruit of the Spirit (love, joy, peace, patience, kindness, goodness, faithfulness, gentleness, self-control) be exhibited more and more in our lives (Galatians 5:22-23).

- May we stand firm against the schemes of the devil, recognizing and resisting Satan in all circumstances (Ephesians 6:10-18; James 4:7; 1 Peter 5:8-10).

- May we not be deceived into unbelief or sin in any form. May we be uncompromising with the world, the flesh, and the devil (Galatians 6:7; Ephesians 5:1-11).

- May we be continually faithful to examine ourselves in light of Scripture—recognizing, confessing, and repenting all inward and outward sins (Psalm 32:1-5; 51:10; Proverbs 28:13; 1 John 1:7-9).

- May we have compassion and be moved when we see the needs of others, as Jesus did (Matthew 9:36).

- May we learn to take up our cross daily, deny ourselves, and follow after You, Lord (Matthew 10:38-39; Mark 8:34).

- May nothing we do be done from "selfish ambition or conceit," but may we consider others better than ourselves (Philippians 2:3 NKJV).

- May we do all things "without complaining or arguing," so that we will be blameless and harmless, "without fault in a crooked and perverse generation" (Philippians 2:14-15 BSB).

- May we "be anxious for nothing," but in thanksgiving let our requests be made known to You, so we can experience Your peace surpassing our understanding and guarding our hearts and minds in You (Philippians 4:6-7 NKJV).

- May we not fear or be discouraged by past failures. May we forget what is behind and reach toward "those things which are ahead," to press on toward the goal for the prize of Your upward call (Philippians 3:12-14 NKJV).[2]

Marriage is an endless sleepover with your favorite weirdo.

UNKNOWN

— 4 —

GOOD
GRIEF

The majority of us have experienced grief in some form or another. It may be impossible to go through life without being acquainted with tragedies of some form, and you might never know how or when grief will enter your story. Additionally, there is no way to know how deeply it will influence you, perhaps even alter portions of who you are and how you deal with your circumstances. Healing from grief has no deadline; it may be long lasting, and you may still feel its effect for years. Sometimes grief sneaks up on you. Perhaps you're watching something on TV or you hear someone share a life experience and are immediately transported to the place of your own painful experience.

As you walk through hardships with your spouse, you'll realize how you grieve differently. Someone may be highly verbal and need to process their emotions out loud; another may need to be quiet and process more internally. Be supportive, gentle, and patient with each other in these times.

As we have walked through seasons of grief ourselves, as well as with friends around us, we have talked about "the new normal." Although every mechanical, mundane task must continue as if nothing ever happened, some aspects of life never go back to what they were before a tragedy. But the tangible nearness of God's presence through these trials supplies us with the blessing of truth for each day, one day at a time. We learn to move to a new rhythm, adjusting as we meander along—perhaps with a limp like Jacob's (Genesis 32:24-32). We cling to God's mercy and love like Jacob wrestled with God and refused to give up until he possessed a blessing from Him.

Step-by-step God gently leads us forward as His promises wash over us and begin to outweigh the pain and overshadow the sorrow. The hope of heaven and eternity gives us strength not to throw in the towel when the throes of pain or sadness overwhelm us. Life is still worth living—and living with joy to the fullest. Hold on to the hope found in the resurrected life of Jesus. He was a man "acquainted with grief" and sorrow (Isaiah 53:3), and yet He overcame death and sin for us. He has paved the way for us to have everlasting life.

Though he slay me, yet will I trust in him.

JOB 13:15 KJV

HEAVENLY GAINS

In the beginning stages of our relationship, I was captivated by Jeremy's unwavering hope in the Lord. It seemed the gravity of his trial and the resolution of his faith went hand in hand. There was a purposefulness about him, albeit from walking through pain, that I hadn't experienced before.

I became equally as intrigued by his first wife, Melissa. He willingly answered me as I bombarded him with questions and tried to wrap my head around their stories of severely raw and real trust.

I felt as though I had been on a search for authentic truth, and some of the puzzle pieces were finally coming together. Everything Jeremy said sank deeply into my heart. I was so spiritually hungry.

He shared about when he first found out Melissa had cancer and went to the hospital to visit her. He had expected to find her disheartened and fearful because of her diagnosis and the daunting road ahead of her, but instead, when he walked into her hospital room, she was beaming. With a heart full of sincerity she told him, "Jeremy, if one person accepts Jesus because of this, it will all be worth it."

Who says that? I am certain you cannot manufacture a heart response like that unless you have a deeply meaningful relationship with the Lord.

Jeremy then told me about a similar occasion when the doctors gave Melissa test results that didn't look very positive. She glanced over at her mom and said, "Mom, what an honor that God thinks I'm faithful enough to walk through this trial."

Jeremy told me of countless times when Melissa was focused on other people around her rather than her own suffering. Her heart broke for the lost, and more than anything she loved to worship Jesus.

Unknowingly, as my love for Jeremy grew, so did my love for Melissa. I was deeply encouraged by her testimony, her faith, and her heart for the Lord. She made a mark on me that remains even to this day. Her death became much more devastating to me as I began to understand the type of woman the Lord had chosen to heal only on heaven's side.

The unwavering faith and love both Melissa and Jeremy had for Jesus was astounding. They were completely sold out for the cause of following Jesus, no matter what it might cost them. And they lived it. It was clear that Jesus came first in their lives, and it was the deepest of loves that united them so sweetly together. They were a fairy tale in every sense of the phrase, except that they were two young people who lived in my time and experienced a genuine life of walking by faith.

I remember sitting in our van at one point, telling my band guys about some of what Jeremy had walked through. I sat back and thought, *Wow, whoever ends up marrying Jeremy, if he ever gets married again, will be so lucky*, not thinking it would be me.

In the middle of our tour in the month of October, when it would have been Melissa's birthday as well as their wedding anniversary, I remember feeling so brokenhearted for my new friend and what he might be going through. I tried my best to comfort him as a friend and to be intentional to check if he was doing okay during the day. A few days later, my band received devastating news about a close friend of ours back home in South Africa who had been murdered for the hubcaps of his car. We were heartbroken. Such depravity was unfathomable, but I immediately felt comforted in knowing that Jeremy knew what it was like to hear life-shaking news.

As our friendship grew toward marriage, there were many times we would weep in each other's arms as we processed the hardest blows life had shot at us. God began healing and knitting us together as we poured out our hearts to each other and carried each other's burdens. Instead of routinely having the "How are you? I'm fine, thanks, and you?" conversation, we would ask each other, "How's your heart?" It sounds cheesy, but it forced us to evaluate and respond on a deeper level. When someone asks you, "How's your heart doing?" you have to stop and think about it. The question set a precedent for transparent communication between us.

Many people have asked me how I'm able to handle my husband talking about another woman—especially so publicly. Before we were married, I had the honor of sitting down with Tammy Courson, also a "second wife." Her husband, John, is a pastor and has often shared the testimony of his first wife and daughter passing away. Tammy asked me, "Would you be okay if Jeremy only ever shared about Melissa and what he went through with her, and never shared about you?" I immediately knew that I would be. I'm not saying it's been a breeze every step of the way, but the Lord has given me the grace to handle it.

I absolutely know that Jeremy's testimony is not about Melissa, but about Jesus. I was deeply impacted when I learned who Jesus was to them, so why should I prevent anyone else from being encouraged by their story? Besides, the Jeremy Melissa married and the Jeremy I married are two different people. Tragedy changes you. Jeremy and I have since walked a road with its own tragedies and triumphs side by side. If God is glorified through my husband's testimony, then I will never stand in the way.

Walls and Doorframes

Years ago, I was reading through the Old Testament (which is really amazing by the way—don't let anyone tell you it isn't), when I came to this passage in Deuteronomy 6:

> Love the LORD your God with all your heart and with all your soul and with all your strength. These commandments that I give you today are to be on your hearts. Impress them on your children. Talk about them when you sit at home and when you walk along the road, when you lie down and when you get up. Tie them as symbols on your hands and bind them on your foreheads. Write them on the doorframes of your houses and on your gates (verses 5-9 NIV).

I was struck by how practical this instruction was—especially the part about writing our love for God on the doorframes of our houses. From then on, I became more intentional about displaying various décor and paintings in our style that had Scripture verses on them. I can't tell you how many times a

passage hanging on my wall has hit the bull's-eye of my heart because it is pertinent to my situation. Scripture truly is God-breathed, living, and active (2 Timothy 3:16; Hebrews 4:12).

Recently, I bought a Magnolia-style (who doesn't love Joanna Gaines?) hanging of 1 Corinthians 13 for our bathroom wall as a checklist. I wanted to ask myself, *Am I being any of these things?* Seldom have I made it past, "Love is patient" (verse 4); patience is an area where I always feel I could grow.

Coincidentally, a few days later Jeremy was being short-tempered and not the kindest husband to me. As we enjoyed a family supper around the dinner table, discussing ways God speaks to us and if there was anything anyone wanted to share, Jeremy confessed to me and the kids that the verse had caught his eye. The Lord had used it to show him he was not loving me well.

I had hoped these verses would be an encouragement to anyone reading them, but little did I know anyone else in the house was paying attention besides me. Without a word from my mouth, my husband heard from the Lord. I had certainly noticed his snappiness with me, and naturally it hurt my feelings, but I didn't have to nag him or point it out. The Holy Spirit revealed it to him for me.

God truly is our best defense and shield. He is the safest place we can run to, and His Word can be trusted. The Holy Spirit is so much better than we are at doing a work in someone or creating a lasting change in them. The sooner we realize that God is the source of everything we need, the better companions we can be to each other.

The Lord was doing an amazing healing work in both of our hearts when we first started spending time together. We often tell people it wasn't that we crossed each other's paths, but instead came alongside each other and continued to run wholeheartedly.

This love of which I speak is slow to lose patience—it looks for a way of being constructive. It is not possessive: it is neither anxious to impress nor does it cherish inflated ideas of its own importance.

Love has good manners and does not pursue selfish advantage. It is not touchy. It does not keep account of evil or gloat over the wickedness of other people. On the contrary, it is glad with all good men when truth prevails.

Love knows no limit to its endurance, no end to its trust, no fading of its hope; it can outlast anything. It is, in fact, the one thing that still stands when all else has fallen.

1 CORINTHIANS 13:4-8 PHILLIPS

According to Christianity, what God values above all is relationship. But for relationship to be meaningful, it must be freely chosen; for relationship to be freely chosen, there must be the possibility of it being rejected; and wherever there is the possibility of rejecting relationship, there is also the possibility of pain and suffering.

VINCE VITALE[1]

EARTHLY LOSSES

There are obvious stages and cycles of grief, but we all have our own unique ways of dealing with it. Because of my testimony about my first wife passing away, numerous people have come up to me over the years, pouring out their stories of hurt and pain and the passing away of their loved ones. As they have shared with me, I've better understood how differently people may grieve. Even if someone has gone through almost the exact same experience I have—for example, losing a wife after a short amount of time—I never say to them, "I totally understand," or, "I know exactly what that's like." In all actuality, I don't know the whole story, the emotional ups and downs they experienced, or every detail of the situation they faced. And even if I did, our emotions and responses as humans are not always alike. We have been given different personalities and have been shaped by our upbringings or cultures, which may cause us to struggle or comprehend hardships in different ways. So when you get married and go through a loss together, don't expect to grieve the same way.

When Adrienne was pregnant with our third child, she had gone in for her fourteen-week checkup when I answered a devastating call from her. I heard her tear-filled voice telling me they couldn't find the baby's heartbeat, and they were going to need to do an ultrasound to confirm their diagnosis. The news hit me like a ton of bricks. Automatically, old memories of loss rose up like a flood. Emotions I hadn't felt since Melissa had gone to be with Jesus hit me hard. *Why would God allow this? Can't He see that I am unable to handle more pain? Can I trust Him to walk me through this again?* Questions such as these invaded my very being.

STAGES OF GRIEF

We've all heard of the five stages of grief: denial, anger, bargaining, depression, and acceptance. They were outlined by psychiatrist Elisabeth Kübler-Ross in her book *On Death and Dying*.[2] She had studied how patients with terminal illnesses react to the news of imminent death, but her theory of the five stages of grief went on to be applied by other experts to the mourners left behind after someone passes away.

More recent studies have shown that not everyone proceeds through these five stages in exactly the same way. Some may speed through them, while others may take years. Some may go through them in order, while others revisit previous stages or jump ahead. And some may skip stages entirely, while others add stages to their experiences with grief.

The danger of thinking we as a society fully understand "how to grieve" is that when each of us reacts differently to similar circumstances, we may judge each other or ourselves for not grieving "correctly."[3] Our guideline from Scripture is that we grieve with heavenly hope (see 1 Thessalonians 4:13).

But God was, as He always is, faithful to reassure me of His goodness and to remind me that He has always provided everything I need to handle any circumstance. I felt His comfort.

Having the tangible love of my life no longer there was a different kind of grief for me than losing our baby, whom I had only been acquainted with for a short amount of time. Therein lay one difference between me and Adrienne. You see, she didn't experience the pit of despair I had felt intensely when Melissa went to heaven, but she would have to deal with the lingering reminder of what once was but now is no more. There were changes in her body, and there were dreams for our family that she had to relinquish whether she wanted to or not.

I remember one day seeing her really downcast. Not clueing in to what was going on (which is not uncommon for me), I had to have her explain that it was close to the time our child was to have been born. I had forgotten about the timeline, so I tried to be tenderhearted toward her, hugged her often, and asked her periodically if she was doing okay. She was still feeling the effects of losing our baby.

There are seasons that have been harder for her as she remains acutely aware of the age gap between the girls and the son who came along later, Egan. She feels the absence of a sibling who would have been much closer to his age. Perhaps from fear of experiencing any form of death again, I had been content to live life with our two girls, Bella and Arie, but Adrienne had still longed for one more. As we prayed together about it, the Lord very quickly changed my heart. I'm so glad He did, because He gave us the sweetest gift in our son, who has the biggest heart and lights up the room wherever he

goes. We love being parents, and our children have been the greatest joys we have ever experienced.

Even though dealing with grief has looked different for both Adrienne and me, we have found that going through hardships together has not only deepened our friendship while we have comforted each other but has also provided a measure of depth and closeness in the relationships we have with people around us that wouldn't be there otherwise. We often refer to this as the "fellowship of the suffering," and as Scripture says, we comfort others with what has comforted us (2 Corinthians 1:3-4).

It's precisely because I feel the problem of suffering so severely that I am led to trust a God who can do something about it.

VINCE VITALE[4]

5

STRESS AND STRAIN

Social media plays a significant role in our daily lives, and all of us present the best versions of ourselves online to friends, family, and the public at large. Couples post perfect pictures together, perhaps while vacationing at a dream destination or going out on a superspecial date night—activities you and your spouse never quite seem to have time to do. Their back-and-forth comments on each other's pages are poetic perfection. You would never think that at home they may be stumbling through hurtful interactions or pushing each other's buttons exactly the same way you push your loved one's. The enemy will whisper, "No way; not them. They would never struggle with that—you're the only dysfunctional couple."

The enemy tries to convince us we're the only ones with our fragilities. And he's smart at his deception, perhaps making us feel embarrassed by our conflicts, resulting in our becoming increasingly isolated and avoiding asking for help. He knows how valuable fellowship with other couples is, especially with those who have gone before us, and he wants to keep us from it.

When we interact with others on a personal level, we can learn from their struggles or varying approaches to relational situations before we face similar tensions of our own. We don't need to discover pitfalls the hard way if someone else can tell us from experience how to avoid them. Or when the inevitable rubs come, others can speak life into our relationships and give us advice, as they may have walked through similar situations.

> Oil and perfume make the heart glad,
> so a man's counsel is sweet to his friend.
>
> PROVERBS 27:9 NASB

There have been moments when we've hung out with other couples and potential conflict situations have arisen. For instance, there was a time when Egan needed tending to, and instead of rushing to the situation himself, Jeremy blamed me for not being attentive to our son. I immediately felt irritated, because caring for Egan was just as much his responsibility as it was mine, but our friends beat me to it and jokingly said, "Bro, you did not just say that to your wife!"

Jeremy immediately recognized his response and laughingly admitted his error. He wasn't defensive or guarded about the criticism he received from them, because it wasn't shared in a moment of contention between him and me. Without causing conflict between us, the Lord used our friends to lightheartedly make Jeremy think about the way he was coming across.

Inviting other people's observations into your relationship can shed light on issues, and sometimes you don't even have to say a word to watch the circumstances change. Oftentimes, the people around you can see your interactions from a different perspective—and perhaps more accurately. When you're willing to be vulnerable, others can get in the gutter with you. They also might have the courage to speak truth to you both, in a way you might not with each other.

It's imperative to surround yourself with people who won't just take your side or always see your point of view. Find friends who will speak truth in love. Give them permission to ask you hard questions that will grow you and challenge you. Don't let your flesh get away with being selfish, operating out of fear, or being harsh or rude. A fight always requires two people—so don't be one of them! Scripture makes it clear: "Make no provision for the flesh" (Romans 13:14). Consider your own heart and its issues. You should be fighting for victory for your marital team—not squaring off against your spouse.

Be accountable—not only to each other, but also to people around you who can speak God's wisdom into your marriage. If you don't have the greatest examples in your community, or if you don't quite have access to the intimate friendships you may want with them, there are many other resources from which you can draw.

Of course, Scripture is full of wisdom, but I have also read biographies of different missionaries and various marriage books and listened to online teachings. I have gleaned so much wisdom through people I have never met by studying their pursuit of Christ and the advice they have given through their writings and lectures. A close community is ideal for accountability, but if for some reason you don't have access to that, commit to pursue wisdom that will put you in step with Jesus.

I highly value the relationships and accountability we have with our closest personal friends. I'm an advocate for Jeremy having "bro time" with his friends the same way I have one-on-one chats with my girlfriends. As men and women, we relate to each other in different ways.

HOSPITALITY TIP

Keep a bag of pasta and can of sauce stocked in your pantry, or perhaps a couple boxes of soup. One of our favorites is roasted red pepper and tomato soup. Having a stocked pantry will give you the freedom to be spontaneous in having people over for a meal.

You don't have to have everything perfectly pulled together. Forget the pressure of an Instagram-worthy setting. I'm not saying there is anything wrong with presenting your home beautifully and creatively, but not everyone is gifted in that area. If unrealistic expectations are holding you back from being in community with others or being hospitable to another couple, then perhaps it's a pressure that needs to be released. Just open your home and invite people in.

Praise be to the God and Father of our Lord Jesus Christ, the Father of compassion and the God of all comfort, who comforts us in all our troubles, so that we can comfort those in any trouble with the comfort we ourselves receive from God.

2 CORINTHIANS 1:3-4 NIV

UNFULFILLING STRATEGIES

Growing up in South Africa, I loved to watch movies about nature and wildlife, especially the majestic African lion. Inevitably I would see the fierce lioness stalk and hunt her prey by isolating them. With speed she would cause confusion, scatter the herd, and strategically lock her sharp eyes on a helpless creature on its own. The animal had little to no chance of surviving the brutal attack and deadly bite of the lioness.

I think the enemy has a similar strategy with us. If he can convince us to isolate ourselves, causing loneliness, we may end up prey to his awful, destructive bite. Although we find ourselves more connected than ever through various forms of technology, there is an upsurge of loneliness in our society as face-to-face interactions become less common. Plus, we have a false expectation of instant fulfillment once we get married. We believe finding our "soul mate" will cure the longings in our souls.

By all means, there is a beautiful and deep companionship that should exist in marriage, but that relationship was never meant to provide the completion for which our hearts hunger. As much as we may want to be in a dreamy and romantic movie scene, hearing something like "You complete me" from the object of our deepest affections, that fantasy is a relationally unattainable ideal. Our spouses will fall far short if we're looking to them to complete our hearts. Only Jesus can do that. We must look to Jesus for our completion, and then all else flows from life in Him.

WHEN HARD TIMES COME

Depression and anxiety deeply affect our society like never before. The overwhelming pressures of life—expectations that are placed on us or that we place on ourselves, emotional and financial strains, and many other stressors—are escalating this epidemic. From 1999 to 2014, the number of Americans taking prescription antidepressants increased by more than 64 percent. [1]

Many people in marriages are facing this very thing and don't know how to deal with it; some spouses may find it hard to walk alongside their loved ones with understanding during these dark times.

Neither Adrienne nor I had ever dealt with severe depression or anxiety in the past. I had experienced a few minor panic attacks and would sometimes feel very down and stressed out, but I'd never had the overwhelming darkness and fear many describe as accompanying depression and anxiety. My feelings always seemed justified by my circumstances. I had heard people describe the immovable heaviness of their situations, but I couldn't quite understand how they couldn't pull themselves out of it. I'd always been able to do so.

Then, a couple years ago, I fell into a deep, dark depression and had panic attacks to go along with it. I was having a rough year. I had been in five different countries in three months with my family and the band, and I had an important radio promotion tour coming up with a full tour following. Someone close to Adrienne and me was battling addiction. The manipulation and deceit intertwined with those choices were tearing apart many aspects of this person's life. The recurring betrayals caused me to distrust someone I never thought I would, and I found that hard to deal with, to say the least.

The stress and heartache bled into many areas of my life. I started struggling to trust the Lord, and as we all know, that distrust affects the very core of our relationship with Him. I started to worry—about something happening to my family, about my future, about juggling my finances. I was exhausted.

Stressful scenarios like those can only go on so long until something breaks, and it did. I remember Adrienne and the kids were out running errands. I was exercising upstairs in our home and suddenly felt like I couldn't breathe. *Is something happening with my heart? Am I going to pass out?*

I realized I was having a panic attack. I'd had a mild one when we were overseas a few weeks before, but I'd thought it was just an isolated event. Well, it came back in full force. In desperation, I called Adrienne while I was trying to catch my breath. It felt like a 100-pound weight was on my chest. I couldn't get enough air in my lungs, and fear overwhelmed me. I thought I was dying. I'm not being dramatic—I plummeted into the pit of depression, and it seemed impossible to fight it. Adrienne came home, and she immediately engaged in constant, bold prayer to wage war on the enemy.

All I could do over the next week was lie in my bed, battling fear and panic in between intervals of weeping. Going out in public was terrifying, but so was being left alone. I wondered if I were losing my mind. At one point, I was lying on Adrienne's lap sobbing uncontrollably, feeling deeply humiliated by how much I was coming unglued. I apologized to her in the midst of it, but she refused to accept my words and would hear nothing of the sort. She insisted this was why we had each other: to hold each other up, pray, and wage spiritual warfare for the ones we love. We prayed constantly, listened to worship music, rebuked the enemy, and pleaded with God to take the panic and depression away.

Life became so dark. Out of nowhere, irrational thoughts about death consumed me. I briefly wondered if God was real, but in the same breath knew in the deepest parts of my heart that He was more real than ever before. I knew that He was the only One able to pull me out of this dark place.

One of the most overwhelming things when you're battling depression is fearing there is no end to where you are. You don't see the light at the end of the tunnel. *How much longer can I fight? Will I survive this?*

In the midst of it all, the Lord began shining a light on my heart. He revealed the hurt and unforgiveness there, the way I was trying to control my circumstances, and—biggest of all—the deep-rooted lack of trust I had in Him. Not until I addressed those things head-on and repented did the anxiety slowly subside. Adrienne and I got on our knees together, poured out our hearts before the Lord, earnestly repented, and continued to cry out to Him for weeks until the darkness was finally gone.

With our busy lifestyles, it's easy to go and go and not dig into what may be going on in the deeper recesses of our hearts. But we need to make a habit of doing that, as David said in the Psalms: "Search me, O God, and know my heart: try me, and know my thoughts: and see if there be any wicked way in me" (139:23-24 KJV). We get so distracted that we don't always see the looming issues hiding below the surface until it's too late.

Sometimes, in the back of my mind, a "barking dog" (as a friend calls it) tries to remind me of what happened and draw my attention to it. The enemy likes to come knocking on our doors to see if the territory still belongs to someone else, or if perhaps he can try gaining ground in our lives again. But we have to remember whom we belong to, resist the enemy, and watch him flee.

I'm not trying to tell you that my brief battle with anxiety and depression has made me an expert. I don't have the formula for you, but I do want you to know how God set me free in this area and what He revealed to my heart. It's the truth we *know* and *believe* that sets us free. Truth in itself will not set us free until we grab hold of it and apply it to our lives and circumstances. We need to walk in a greater understanding of God's love for us and our identities in Him. God set me free in this area, and I believe He can liberate you too. I'm fully aware there are chemical and hormonal imbalances perhaps requiring medication, and many people have not found victory for years. But please don't give up. If you are dealing with this in your relationship, it's okay to ask for help. Seek counsel; seek Jesus.

Adrienne doesn't struggle with fear or anxiety. She doesn't know what it's like to walk through depression, but she still battled alongside me and got in the trenches with all her heart. She would ask me, "What do you need me to do? Pray? Worship? Simply lie next to you? Read Scripture?" She never put pressure on me or enforced a time frame for when my freedom or breakthrough should come; she fought, not knowing the outcome. Not only did she fight for me privately through prayer, but she spurred me to fight.

The fear of God overcomes all other fears. Anxiety is overcome by faith in God, and spiritual attacks are overcome by worshiping God in our daily walk.

NEIL T. ANDERSON
AND RICH MILLER[2]

God incarnate is the end of fear;
and the heart that realizes that
He is in the midst, that takes heed
to the assurance of His loving
presence, will be quiet in the midst
of alarm. "No weapon formed
against you will prosper, and every
tongue that rises against you in
judgment will be condemned."
Only be patient and be quiet.

F.B. MEYER[3]

WHEN LOVE GOES COLD

Unconditional love—is it really possible? Perhaps this is what Paul was talking about when he instructed men to love their wives as Jesus loves His church (Ephesians 5:25). The love Jesus has for His church is faithful, purifying, patient, and certainly unconditional. Oftentimes, because we don't understand something in Scripture or we think it seems unattainable, we let

God's Word fall to the wayside and consider it no longer relevant. But God wants us to study and apply the hard parts of His Word, not ignore them.

The way Jesus loves us is based on who He is, not on our works or how well we have it all together. If we are to love each other as He loves us, we should not withhold our love or affection when our spouses aren't performing up to our expectations or when we're tired of the places they have been stuck for so long.

"He should be beyond this by now!"

"She should know by now!"

Your feelings and thoughts may be absolutely valid, but God gives us all we need to walk with each other in a manner that brings unity instead of distance. Such unlimited devotion may seem absolutely beyond your abilities at times, especially the longer you stay married. And the truth is, it *is* beyond you! Your natural well of love will run desperately dry apart from being filled with Jesus.

If we love only those we deem worthy of it, every one of us would go without.

But if we entrust our abilities to love each other to the Lord first, then based on His supernatural character at work in us, we can learn to love above our human capacity. His love is based on who He is and His commitment to His own character. His love is unconditional, and He cannot deny Himself.

Have you ever thought about what it's like to be married to you?

Imagine if we were to approach marriage the same way: *Based on my commitment and openness to God, and based on His Spirit alive in me, I'm able to love you. Not because you measure up, and not because you deserve it, even though that would make it much easier and certainly more convenient. But because my heart is overflowing from my connection to Jesus, love spills over to you.*

The secret is Christ in me, not me in a different set of circumstances.

ELISABETH ELLIOT[5]

When I pray for another person, I am praying for God to open my eyes so that I can see that person as God does, and then enter into the stream of love that God already directs toward that person.

PHILIP YANCEY[6]

same thing about you. How they raise their children, fix their meals, communicate, and celebrate together develops out of their own culture and life together. Their history and experiences are not yours, so don't judge other couples by an artificial preference you set. This does not mean excusing dysfunctional, unhealthy, unbalanced, or abusive behavior. But it does mean not judging quirky personalities. We are all weirdos in one way or another.

QUIZ

Ask each other these questions, then talk about your answers. No judgment, no comparisons—just honesty and unconditional love. No matter how long you've been married, you're sure to learn something about each other.

- What may contribute to your "getting up on the wrong side of the bed"?
- What's one thing you wish I'd do more often?
- What's one thing you wish I'd stop doing?
- What does a relaxing day spent with me look like to you?
- When and where do you feel the most peaceful?
- Do you need more or less "alone time"?
- Is there anything you've missed doing since we got married?
- Is there anything new you wish we would do together?

Don't compare your marriage to others' either. The grass may seem greener on your neighbor's lawn, but you don't know what goes on behind closed doors. No matter whom you marry, you will have to deal with someone's sinful human nature. Tend to your own marriage. Weed your own garden, prune your own trees, plant the perennials in your yard that will come back year after year—stronger, fuller, and more beautiful. Every hard winter makes the spring abundantly more beautiful. Every season you weather together will shape the two of you into one.

6

MATERIAL
MATTERS

Money is a factor in any marriage, no matter how much or little is in the bank. Unfortunately, financial strain is one of the leading causes of marriage breakdowns. Spouses need to have similar priorities when it comes to using their money, agreeing on the big and small purchases. When they have a unified plan, it is easier for them to stay out of debt, and living debt free means having the flexibility to follow God's leading joyously.

About ten years ago, we had difficult tenants in our rental house. For the first few months, our renters were fine; they paid on time, and everything seemed great. But all of a sudden it became a nightmare to get payments from them. There was excuse after excuse, even handwritten notes in our mailbox pleading for forgiveness and not to be evicted. We found out they had been breeding dogs in our home and caused more than $40,000 worth of damage. The neighbors had reported them to the police because of house parties, and as you can imagine, there were damages from those parties as well. We were in shock. We had given in to their initial pleas for grace and had tried to work with them, but it turned out the husband was a scam artist who later ended up in prison when his other shenanigans finally caught up with him.

Recently, we went through a similar situation with another unethical renter. It wasn't as bad this time, but this tenant used constant manipulation and deceit, all the while making excuses—but no payments.

Both of these families claimed to be believers and played the "grace card." But they weren't looking for grace or mercy or even forgiveness from us; they wanted to break their contracts, live for free as long as possible, and have zero consequences. These situations really bothered us. How could someone so brazenly take advantage of another believer? How could a Christian manipulate God's gift of grace for earthly gain?

We had a choice to make: We could stay offended, letting our emotions run wild while our possessions kept a hold on us—or we could give everything over to the Lord and trust Him to repay what was taken. It was a reminder that our possessions are ultimately the Lord's, and we are just stewards of what He has put in our hands. He can repay what was stolen or cheated from us. If someone has taken something from us and He wants it back in our hands, He'll put it there. Instead of letting our hearts and heads get cluttered with resentment, frustration, or gossip when we are wronged, we can experience freedom and rest in the Lord.

FAST FACTS FROM DAVE RAMSEY

- Money is the number-one issue married couples argue about.
- 41 percent of those married five years or less say they felt pressured to spend more than they could afford on their wedding. Over half (54 percent) of couples married five years or less say some of their wedding expenses were covered with a credit card—and 73 percent of those couples say they regret that decision.
- Nearly two-thirds of all marriages start off in debt. 43 percent of couples married more than 25 years started off in debt, while 86 percent of couples married five years or less started off in the red—twice the number of their older counterparts.
- One-third of people who say they argued with their spouse about money say they hid a purchase from their spouse because they knew their partner would not approve.
- 94 percent of respondents who say they have a "great" marriage discuss their money dreams with their spouse, compared to only 45 percent of respondents who say their marriage is "okay" or "in crisis." 87 percent of respondents who say their marriage is "great" also say they and their spouse work together to set long-term goals for their money.
- 63 percent of those with $50,000 or more in debt feel anxious about talking about their personal finances. Almost half (47 percent) of respondents with consumer debt say their level of debt creates stress and anxiety.[1]

Possessions and wealth will never satisfy. Prominence and importance will never satisfy. Optimal health and fitness will never satisfy. Job promotions and opportunities will never satisfy. Every fulfilled dream and desire for life and relationships will never satisfy. Only when we find ourselves fulfilled in Jesus will we find true satisfaction in this life.

> I have learned to be content whatever the circumstances. I know what it is to be in need, and I know what it is to have plenty. I have learned the secret of being content in any and every situation, whether well fed or hungry, whether living in plenty or in want.
>
> PHILIPPIANS 4:11-12 NIV

BUILDING AN ETERNAL HOME

It's not wrong to be rich, and it's not wrong to be poor. Adrienne and I have experienced both extremes. Neither one of us grew up in wealthy homes; we both had our fair share of hand-me-downs and powdered milk. As young adults, we had little to no income. I lived off canned tuna fish and ramen noodles, and Adrienne survived on ramen noodles and frozen vegetables.

God has used times of struggle—financial and otherwise—to teach me plenty of things. When I was on the lower end of the financial spectrum, I needed a practical faith, believing that God would supply my physical needs. Now that He has trusted me with more than just my daily bread, I must be far more intentional in seeking God's vision for how to steward what He has put into my hands. Both circumstances require prayer and faith. Neither is a godlier status than the other. The Holy Spirit spoke to Adrienne's heart one day as she was praying and said, "It doesn't matter whether it's big or small, but whether God gets the glory in it all."

Along with the financial extremes themselves, we have also experienced the pendulum swing of people's responses to the wealth and success we now have. On one side, there are those who believe it is wrong and materialistic to be wealthy; on the other side are those who believe money is the physical evidence of being in God's will, and therefore, they believe those who struggle financially are not right with Him.

Whether you're financially established or not, finances are an idol in your life if they consume your thoughts and habits or come before your relationship with the Lord. If you're constantly focused on how little you have and how hard life is, then your focus is off. If you're constantly focused on how much you have and how much more you want, then your focus is off.

It's the *love* of money that is "the root of all evil" and causes sorrows—not the possession and use of money itself. Our intention, no matter our financial status, should be to pursue righteousness, godliness, faith, love, patience, and meekness (1 Timothy 6:10-11 KJV).

> How do you steward what God puts in your hands, whether slim pickings or plenty?

Don't let your possessions define you. Although an affluent, prosperous life is highly praised in Western culture, our motivation should be different as followers of Christ. How much or how little we have shouldn't define our worth, neither should it characterize what we chase after.

I'm not claiming we get this right all the time, but Adrienne and I have held each other accountable over the years to balance what we spend on ourselves with sowing into things of eternal worth—things that don't benefit us personally or from which we won't see an earthly reward. We hold on to our possessions lightly, practicing hospitality and generosity. Oftentimes, the Holy Spirit will nudge us to commit to giving toward different ministries or missionaries. We have prayed and asked the Lord to put specific families on our hearts and even specific amounts—and almost every time we have come back thinking the exact same thing, or at least very close.

Do not lay up for yourselves treasures on earth, where moth and rust destroy and where thieves break in and steal; but lay up for yourselves treasures in heaven, where neither moth nor rust destroys and where thieves do not break in and steal. For where your treasure is, there your heart will be also.

MATTHEW 6:19-21 NKJV

We have also tried to be intentional about including our kids in experiencing the reward of giving to others. Years ago, during Christmastime, we went out to eat as a family and decided to secretly pay for someone else's meal. We prayed together that the Lord would show us who needed it the most and then asked our server to help us pull it off. It was a joy to see how excited our kids were, and our family talked about it for hours afterward, each looking forward to hearing the other family's backstory when we get to heaven one day.

GIVING BACK

Have you ever judged the outside circumstances of another and wondered, *Why should I work hard to benefit people who have been completely negligent or unwise? Why is it my job to bail them out?* No one is saying it is your job, but if either you or your spouse are feeling a stirring to be generous by helping someone in the situation where they have landed themselves, be willing to listen to each other. Perhaps the Lord is putting something specific on your partner's heart, and you need to invite Him into the middle of the conversation. What is God's heart for the matter?

If you and your spouse don't see eye to eye about giving, then pray together and ask the Lord for direction. Ask Him for a scripture or a word of confirmation. Don't just presume either one of you knows the exact "right thing to do." Just as God could feed His people with manna (Exodus 16), never-dry last jars of flour and oil (1 Kings 17:11-16), or a measly five loaves and two fish (Matthew 14:13-21), He doesn't necessarily meet our needs the same way every time.

We have learned that sometimes the Lord allows people to go through hardships—financial and otherwise—in order to teach them. If we constantly bail each other out, we could be hindering the refining work He wants to do in our lives—the circumstances which might cause us to cry out to Him. However, the Lord could use your generosity to pull someone out of the pit and reveal His love to them, or perhaps He simply wants you to bear their burdens in prayer.

Heed your spouse's thoughts. God has given you to each other for a reason. There are times to make big purchases on other people's behalf, and there are times to keep your wallet in your pocket.

> Be prayerful. Honor the Lord with your finances. Put Him first in everything.

We, as a family, believe in giving back to the Lord. Call it our "firstfruits"; call it "tithing"; call it whatever you want. We gladly put God first and honor Him with our wealth. We trust He will provide what we need.

As Jesus observed with the poor widow giving her pitiful two coins while the wealthy gave large offerings (Mark 12:41-44), it's not about how much you give, but whether or not you are giving your all. She gave everything she had, not just from her abundance. Although her gift was the least, Jesus accredited it as the greatest.

CHECKS AND BALANCES

When our daughter Bella was much younger, after she had overheard Adrienne and me talking about my upcoming touring schedule, she pulled me aside with much concern and said, "Daddy, you don't have to work so much. We have everything we need." It stopped me in my tracks and forced me to make sure that my motivation for doing what I do was to expand the Lord's kingdom and not my own, and that I wasn't sacrificing time with my family for my own selfish gain. Her innocent observation has since stayed in the back of my mind as a way for me to check my heart.

Is the world a better place because you live in it? Is your home a better place? Don't overwork to have more money and end up missing out on the relationships with the very ones you are providing for.

If your family is struggling with debt, then it may be right for you to invest more time at work in the short term. But let your family help by living frugally at home until you reach your goals. Don't be embarrassed by the restraint you show in spending while making wise financial decisions. Don't worry about how your friends down the road are spending their money. Don't hide purchases from your spouse. How do you suppose that will work out in the long run? Keep your end goal in mind and work together to get there.

A recent survey found that about 90 percent of the millennials who responded think social media creates a peer-pressure environment that encourages them to keep up with their friends. Don't be the one who spends too much simply because it makes you feel good in the moment to buy everyone gifts or pay for everyone's meals. Don't try to make yourself look better by bragging about doing things you can't afford to do. That hubris serves no one. If you don't have the money, don't spend it.

Our son, Egan, loves to make bets with people. He enjoys the playful game and interaction with others. One day he came home and confessed he owed a friend 17 dollars! We found out he had bet money he didn't have and wound up with a debt that someone else (that is, we—his parents) would have to cover. Luckily, Egan's young creditor was a good friend, and so we took the opportunity to explain to both of them how dangerous the habit of betting can be. Sure, at age seven this is a silly, seemingly harmless amount of money to lose, but what might this scenario look like fast-forwarded?

Make sure you live within your means as a family, and don't have a spending budget that exceeds your finances. For the most part, we try avoiding debt, besides our mortgage.

The Eternal Cost of Debt

It is safe to say that America is not a pay-as-you-go society. In 2018, Americans spent $113 billion on credit card interest alone. Quite simply, interest is money paid for purchasing goods and services early—before the card holders have earned the dollars necessary to trade for them. Even debit-card holding, cash-only payers threw away money on interest in the US fiscal year 2018, as some of their taxes went toward paying off the $371 billion in interest on the national debt. In both the personal and national cases, interest payments went toward nothing tangible—the goods and services themselves are yet to be paid for, though long-ago consumed—because interest pays for the luxury of immediacy. It lets us take what we want right now, before we have a right to do so.

What if that combined $484 billion (that has bought literally nothing) had been put to use? Americans could have done one of the following:

- sent 3.3 billion young women to secondary school [5]
- dug 60.5 million new wells across Africa [6]
- built 34 energy-producing nuclear fusion reactors in France [7]
- rebuilt Iraq *more than five times* [8]
- paid all US cancer patients' direct medical costs, *six times each* [9]

Let's stop using the money we earn today to pay for yesterday's purchases when we could be investing in tomorrow's people.

Is anyone thirsty?

Come and drink—even if you have no money!

Come, take your choice of wine or milk—it's all free!

Why spend your money on food that does
not give you strength?

Why pay for food that does you no good?

Listen to me, and you will eat what is good.

You will enjoy the finest food.

Come to me with your ears wide open.

Listen, and you will find life.

I will make an everlasting covenant with you.

I will give you all the unfailing love I
promised to David.

ISAIAH 55:1-3 NLT

TEACHING VALUE

Even though I am the main breadwinner, Adrienne and I make our financial decisions together. She understands the weight and pressure that I carry as the primary provider, and I am supportive of the role she plays as the stay-at-home parent. Our family couldn't survive without both of us, so we value each other's insight and opinions. Even with our differing personalities and spending habits, we still take time to hear each other's points of view and to talk through our long-term plans for the future. There have been situations where we've both added valuable thoughts and insight into the best way forward as we have discussed goals and the future of our finances. Even though I am more of a "numbers person" than Adrienne, she has great perspective and can think of things I haven't.

FAST FACT

An average stay-at-home parent would be paid more than $178,000 in the marketplace each year for services such as teaching, cooking, coaching, and administrating.[10]

We have learned to differentiate between our wants and needs. We're also teaching our kids the same lesson. It's important for us to find the balance between blessing our kids and not buying them everything they want. When they really want something that is unnecessary but not harmful, then we try to help them earn it through their own hard work. They may

complain for days and weeks, but the time it takes them to earn that item and accomplish that goal establishes a strong work ethic. It would be a disservice to give them everything now and let them only start learning the value of things when they enter the adult world.

Our girls wanted to go on a mission trip to Uganda, and instead of us just paying for it on the spot, we encouraged them to work for it. They were so motivated and took hold of any opportunity they could. They did chores, babysat, cooked and sold meals for friends, sang at events, and made jewelry to earn money for their trip. The experience gave them a sense of how hard people have to work to raise or earn money, and they felt the joy of accomplishment when they reached their goal. It also gave them an appreciation for the constant hard work we do as parents. Overall, it was a highly valuable life lesson.

As you navigate life together as husband and wife, talk through financial issues with each other. If and when it is appropriate, include your children in those conversations so they can learn alongside you. Keep in mind that we brought nothing into this world, and we cannot take anything out of it (1 Timothy 6:7). Leave a legacy of faith through who you are and what you do, not just a financial inheritance.

There is treasure to be desired and oil in the dwelling of the wise; but a foolish man spendeth it up. He that followeth after righteousness and mercy findeth life, righteousness, and honour.

PROVERBS 21:20-21 KJV

Wisdom is a defense as money is a defense, but the excellence of knowledge is that wisdom gives life to those who have it.

ECCLESIASTES 7:12 NKJV

Do not worry, saying, "What shall we eat?" or "What shall we drink?" or "What shall we wear?" For the pagans strive after all these things, and your Heavenly Father knows that you need them. But seek first the kingdom of God and His righteousness, and all these things will be added unto you.

MATTHEW 6:31-33 BSB

TIGHT-BUDGET DATING

Don't think that date night ends once you are married. Prioritize just-the-two-of-you time! You don't have to spend a lot of money to get a lot of benefit from your time together. The key is making the evening special. Here are a few ideas for keeping things cheap:

1. Have date night in a secluded room. Include your kids—it will be good for them to see you prioritizing each other. They can wait on your table and do the dishes. Don't forget to tip!
2. Check your city's calendar and attend a free-admission night at your local museum. Many will provide complimentary refreshments.
3. Pack a picnic—make it as simple or as fancy as you'd like—and hike to a quiet spot.
4. Take advantage of discount-finder apps and check your local restaurants' social media sites for deals.

— 7 —

US OVER ME

When two individuals become one in marriage, compromises are required. But what happens when one or both partners wonder, *Am I reaching my full potential?* or, *Am I keeping my spouse from reaching his or hers?* God may use you differently once you are a spouse and parent, so don't constantly judge yourself and others against the goals and achievements of the past. God wants us working together for His kingdom, not blazing trails by ourselves.

MADE FOR RELATIONSHIP

The nature of love is God Himself; He *is* love (1 John 4:8). God is also in eternal community; He is in an endless love relationship in the Trinity—Father, Son, and Holy Spirit. Relationship is His very being.

God made us in His image, which means we were made for relationship—first with Him, then with others. He wants us to look like Him and experience the fullness of His love, to honor one another and give the gift of relationship to each other. As we grow together and are patient with each other, we will see His beautiful, continuous work in our lives.

But the love we have to offer each other is incomplete. Because of our humanity, we each enter marriage with deficits that cannot be covered by the strengths of a partner who comes up short equally but differently. There may be ways we can balance each other out, but we most certainly can't complete each other, no matter how romantic that notion might sound to some. The only way we can love each other well and completely is in a supernatural union that includes the source of love Himself.

Christianity is vastly different from any other religion in this way. Every other religion requires believers to improve themselves first. Only as they improve can they be elevated in spirituality. But Christianity is God reaching down to us in our dirty, unworthy state. God demonstrates His love by making a way, time and time again, for us to have relationship with Him. He perfectly loved us before we ever loved Him, and He will never love us any more or less in any other season of our lives. His love is preemptive, sacrificial, and unselfish.

But we as Christians have let too much of the world's thinking infiltrate our own. We view relationships the way the world does—as self-serving. We expect from relationships what the world expects—satisfaction and bringing out the best in ourselves. *You make me happy; you fulfill my needs;*

> # *The kingdom is better when we're together.*
> ## JONATHAN AND WYNTER PITTS[1]

you see to it that I reach my full potential. But relationships are polar opposite in God's kingdom.

God's love is unconditional. He comes alongside us and is our strength in our weaknesses. When we expect others to love us in a way only God can, we end up destroying ourselves and them, because perfect love is impossible without God for imperfect humans.

We have to understand that God is the very One who created marriage. He is the One who outlined what it should be. However much we try to explain it, there is something supernatural about two people becoming one flesh. It is just as holy and mysterious as the compound unity of the Trinity—

God's very nature of relationship represented in our marriages. And it is just as impossible to undo. If we have flawed theology about who God is and don't understand His nature and role in our marriages, then we ignore the very One who holds them together.

Lord Jesus, we put our relationship in Your hands. Since You are the great designer and maker of all things, since You are love itself, please give us the ability to walk in humility and make the daily exchange of our fleshly desires for Your perfection. Help us walk supernaturally and unselfishly where we feel weak and have been seeking our own gain. Help us not look to the world for our narrative, but to You. Please do a work in our hearts so we love each other as You love us. Amen.

Do you find yourself misunderstanding God's integral place in your marriage covenant? Do you expect relationships to fulfill your own needs instead of going to the source of love Himself? Ask Him to teach you and give you what you need. Don't think you're pulling the wool over God's eyes; He already knows your need. Why not make the great exchange with Him? His love for your selfishness. His patience for your harshness. His tenderness and grace for your frustrations.

Love at first is a child,
and grows stronger by age.

JOHN NEWTON[2]

BABY ON THE WAY, NOT IN THE WAY

Husbands, be patient with your wives when they are overwhelmed. Mothering is one of the most exhausting jobs on the planet. Having a constant tagalong every single time you use the restroom or shower can wear you down after a while. The demands can seem never ending, and the hope of a break may easily evaporate, along with the hopes of having nicely folded laundry, a clean kitchen, and a spotlessly vacuumed home. There are vic-

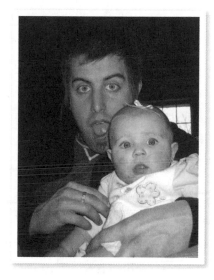

torious days here and there when the long to-do list gets completely checked off—which then lose their glory in a tornado of toys, crumbs, laundry, and dishes all needing full attention again. How does this mass chaos happen so quickly? However many times you do the chores, they just don't stay done!

So don't judge your wife when she rolls into bed at night, exhausted and wiped out. A mother has completed the jobs of a referee, teacher, chef, house cleaner, nurse, friend, cheerleader, coach, taxi driver, launderer, and police-woman—most likely all in a day—while hearing her name called somewhere close to a thousand times every hour. Be tender.

And wives, as much as you feel overwhelmed and exhausted from your never-ending responsibilities, remember that your husband carries an enormous amount of weight as well. Don't just dump the baby in his hands when he walks through the front door, saying, "It's your turn now!"

Depending on what your husband does for work, he could be coming home from exhausting all-day meetings, supervising different programs or difficult people, creating projects to meet urgent deadlines, answering tons of e-mails all needing a response *immediately*, or making hundreds of executive decisions for the people around him—while bearing the pressures of providing for his family and maybe desiring to be respected as a great leader.

When I first became a mom to our Bella, I had to adjust to many changes, at times feeling as if I might drown in the depths of diapers. I was eager to do something outside the home, but it seemed impossible. We were a part of a small church community in Lafayette, Indiana, where Jeremy's parents pastor. There were so many needs at the church and so few people to fill them. One day I was talking to my mom-in-law, Teri, about these needs and how much I wanted to fill them, and yet I didn't have the time or capacity to do so. She reminded me that there are seasons for everything. Just because there is a need doesn't mean I have to be the one to fill it. I learned to focus on the things only I could fulfill—especially in motherhood.

Your season with your little ones—as all-consuming as it is, especially the first few years—flies by so fast. Before you know it, your "baby" is driving. (Jeremy and I will soon be drawing straws for who "gets" to teach driving lessons!) I'm not saying you can't do anything besides be a mom or dad; there have been humongous and demanding projects on both of our plates during every season of our lives. We all must learn to balance the seasons and hold plans loosely.

Even when you both feel like everyone wants or needs something from you, remember that the seasons will change. This is not your eternity. Your kids will graduate and move out of the house, and you don't want to end up just being roommates with your spouse. Don't neglect your marriage; that relationship needs to outlast the season of parenting young kids.

How can fathers balance staying supportive and secure in their relationships with their wives and not be jealous of the attention mothers give their kids? How can mothers pay attention to their husbands, even when the children are so much more demanding of their time? How can you serve each other? Obviously not every family's dynamic includes a stay-at-home mom and a working dad. There are many moms who work as well, and some of them are the main breadwinners for their family. Every couple has different preferences for how they handle different seasons and what they need from each other in order to be regularly refreshed. Work it out together. Recognize you both have needs and desires and meet in the middle, whatever your scenario looks like.

We can slip into bad thought patterns when we are too zoomed in on our own lives. We see everything close up and can become overwhelmed by the blurry details that don't always make sense in the moment.

Ask the Lord to help you take a step back in order to see the bigger picture. Know every season has its purpose, and nothing should be wished away. For me, the more time goes by, the more I see how God has groomed my family for certain chapters of life by allowing us to walk through situations that didn't quite make sense in the moment. So let's trust God as we follow His lead. He truly does weave masterpieces of our lives if we let Him.

We can also trust God with our spouses. There have been many times I have rested in Him, knowing Jeremy hears His voice and, in the right time, the Lord will speak and do a work in his heart. Who am I to determine what life lessons my significant other should have learned by now? Do I think I have mastered everything myself? I think not. As I wait and surrender my trust to God to do His work in His timing for my spouse, He works in my heart at the same time. Spouses need to pray for each other and deal with each other patiently, knowing that God teaches us all in different ways and at different times.

What is God teaching you right now? Why don't you ask your spouse the same question? Instead of being frustrated with the place they're in, you may find you have more middle ground than you think.

> I have told you these things, so that in me you may have peace. In this world you will have trouble. But take heart! I have overcome the world.
>
> JOHN 16:33 NIV

NO *I* IN *TEAM*

Are you jealous of your spouse's success? Do you feel as if you're always in the shadows? No matter what season of life you're in, remember that you're running this race together. Your spouse may be the lead runner now, but there will be times when they finish a leg of the race and hand off the baton to you. You're not running against each other. God has placed you together for a reason. Always be encouraging to each other—no matter what your role is. It takes a team to build something.

Be intentional about sharing the details of your day and inviting your spouse into where you are. Think through what you can do practically to ensure you're on the same team. One small way Adrienne and I share life together is by sharing an email address. It sounds insignificant and can often be a little overwhelming, but it helps us stay on track with what's going on in each other's lives from an external point of view, especially since communicating details is not my strong point.

A fun thing we have done in different seasons is chosen a TV series to watch together after we have put the kids to bed. Adrienne grew up watching sports with her dad, and so she loves to watch sports with me as well. Because we often spend days apart from each other when I'm touring, we make an effort to stay connected and cheer for each other (not just our favorite teams!).

ANGER AS AN INDICATOR

Never neglect each other and let resentment simmer under the surface. Words spoken in anger will not produce the fruit you want. Anger itself is not the problem; it's what you do with it.

When Bella and Arie were toddlers, I met a friend for lunch at Chick-fil-A. We were sitting inside the play area, chatting while the kids climbed and ran around. The next thing I knew, another mom was crouched down, yelling in Bella's face for apparently taking her son's toy. Poor Bella was in complete shock while this woman unleashed total madness on my daughter, grabbed her child, and stormed out of the restaurant.

I instantly became angry and protective. What kind of adult is so out of control that she yells in a little kid's face? Now, my kids are not perfect, but stealing a stranger's toy sounded completely out of character for Bella. I waited to hear what the real story was. Apparently, the boy started crying because he couldn't reach the toy he dropped, and Bella had reached down to give it back to him. The mom had wrongly presumed she had grabbed the toy out of his hands.

I was fuming, to say the least, but I felt the help of the Holy Spirit restraining me from chasing after the mom to give her a lesson on how inappropriate her actions were. My friend was blown away that I didn't freak out at the woman for what she did, but what good would it have done?

It's best to leave crazy people alone. Don't fight fire with fire.

The Bible tells us that Jesus never sinned, and yet there were a few times in Scripture when He was angry. Anger is an emotion God has created us

> *In your anger do not sin.*
>
> EPHESIANS 4:26 NIV

to feel. Understandably, anger has a bad rap in our culture. There are many times we should have way more self control than we do, especially in confrontational circumstances. Yet, undealt-with and suppressed anger results in unhealthy explosions. So pray through anger; talk through it. Recognize when heat is rising in your heart. There should be no excuses for letting anger and irrationality take over.

When I feel angry, I try to pay attention to *why*. Sometimes my feelings indicate that a boundary of some kind has been crossed. I then ask the Holy Spirit to show me what's in my heart that needs His attention. Oftentimes, by doing this, the Lord has shown me an area needing to be talked through or to receive His healing touch. Ask God to be the revealer of your heart and show you the root of your feelings—and give Him access to all areas. Nothing should be off limits to Him.

Marriage is hard. There are no two ways about it. It doesn't matter whom you marry; there will be a clash of wills at some point in time. Never mind the fact that, as it is, men and women are so different from each other. Throw in two different personalities, being raised in two different homes or perhaps different cultures, and you're certain to have conflict waiting for you around any corner. Choose to believe the best about each other, and share what God is doing in your hearts and lives.

JOYOUS TRIALS

> Consider it pure joy, my brothers, when you encounter trials of many kinds, because you know that the testing of your faith develops perseverance. Allow perseverance to finish its work, so that you may be mature and complete, not lacking anything (James 1:2-4 BSB).

What does it mean to consider trials "pure joy"? Was James crazy? Joy in trials? This struck me one day. I realized that this type of joy comes when you value the character developing in your heart more than being comfortable and avoiding trials. It's like saying, "I'll take the pain—no matter how much it hurts—because the reward of deep, godly character developing in me is more valuable to me."

I'm the chief of being willing to undergo pain in physical areas, especially when it comes to working out or being disciplined about my health. I love pushing myself hard when I work out. I'll run until I throw up, get amped about feeling my muscles burn, but I'm much slower to be full of joy when it comes to allowing my character to be shaped through a trial. Trials can be exhausting and stretching, and most of the time I would rather just not deal with them.

The truth is, diamonds are shaped under pressure, and pearls come from irritants. There's no way to develop inner beauty and depth of character without going through hardships, and the same is true for our relationships. When I look back at the years Adrienne and I have been together, we have clung to Jesus and each other during the trials we have faced. Instead of separating us, those trials have solidified our friendship and drawn us closer together. Because of the hardships, we have forged the best friendship, and I couldn't imagine going through life with anyone else. We know trials will come in the future, but instead of each being alone, we can lean on each other.

Blessed is the man who perseveres under trial, because when he has stood the test, he will receive the crown of life that God has promised to those who love Him.

JAMES 1:12 BSB

PRAYER

Lord Jesus, please help us stand united in the changing seasons of our life together. Help us give each other the benefit of the doubt in the middle of our exhaustion and as we juggle the various responsibilities we have. Help us build our marriage and not tear it down—and teach us how to look for ways we can be a support to each other. Help us not look to our own interests, but to each other's. Help us be mature and forgiving when we fall short and push each other's buttons so that our marriage can be a blessing to us, to our family, and to those in community with us. Amen.

— 8 —

HE'S STRONG, SHE'S STRONG

Husbands and wives are to live as one together in Christ, sharing equal value and honor and mutually submitting to each other "out of reverence for Christ" (Ephesians 5:21). We should strive for oneness and not dominate or manipulate each other. Although marriage is a beautiful companionship of two complementary counterparts, each with different and unique strengths to bring to the table, Scripture is clear about putting God at the head of the family, followed by the husband and then the wife (verse 23).

The buck has to stop with the husband. But his leadership doesn't give him the right to be a controlling dictator or to lead by strong-arming; Jesus taught us that the greatest will be a servant of all (Mark 9:35). Just as Jesus submitted Himself to the Father, we submit ourselves to one another. This type of partnership will bring balance and peace to our homes.

YOU'RE HOLDING ME BACK!

If you're thinking marriage is hard, then you're right—it is. But the depth of companionship you experience when you're in right relationship with one another is unparalleled by anything in this world. This presents a dilemma, though, because the only way to get there is by relinquishing your singleness, which may include certain dreams, desires, or aspirations. Essentially, you're dying to yourself as you build a new union with new life goals by serving each other and laying your life down for each other—mutually submitting. Any other path you try to take is self-serving and will not create the marriage or relationship you actually want.

You cannot change your significant other; only God can accomplish that. If, as men and women, we're trying to prove we can each do the other's job better, then we miss the very essence of who we're supposed to be in the first place. God designed us differently for a reason. If you're a woman, be all woman. If you're a man, be all man. We both bring different views and insights to the table that are valuable. When in unison, they complement each other and work well together.

We are in desperate need of strong kingdom men and strong kingdom women in our society who are willing to work together instead of competing against one another—who are willing to love and respect and recognize the value of each of our positions. Be who you are to the fullest of who God has called you to be in the place where He has put you.

Enjoy each season you experience together. Neither one of you will be the same person you started out as in your marriage. Let the Lord be the cord that binds you together. Since He instituted marriage, He is also the One who knows the way it works best.

> The eye cannot say to the hand, "I have no need of you," nor again the head to the feet, "I have no need of you"... But God has so composed the body, giving greater honor to the part that lacked it, that there may be no division in the body, but that the members may have the same care for one another. If one member suffers, all suffer together; if one member is honored, all rejoice together.
>
> 1 CORINTHIANS 12:21, 24-26

DEAR LADIES, LET'S DEFINE *STRONG*

When the disciples heard Jesus' explanation and emphasis on the commitment of marriage, their response was, "It is better not to marry" (Matthew 19:10). They knew marriage would require a lot from them, enough to make them second-guess if the relationship was worth the required time and effort.

Anything worthwhile should have a high price. King David was fully aware of this when he prepared to make his worship offering to God in 2 Samuel 24:24. A man wanted to provide David everything he needed for his sacrifice, but the king responded, "I will not offer burnt offerings to the LORD my God that cost me nothing." The value of an object is the price paid for it. And the only way to be a support to your husband is to give of yourself. A great marriage will have a price tag on it.

Wives are described in Scripture as *helpmates* or *partners*, someone who comes alongside her husband. What would the purpose of this design be? Would it be to see each other stagnate or be slow to mature? To tear each other down through a lack of respect? To take charge whenever your husband doesn't? No, husbands and wives are in this life together to champion each other in reaching their full potential. Neither one should be a doormat, but you should have mutual respect for each other. A win for your husband is a win for you, and vice versa.

In our culture, have we come to prefer domineering women? If you put your mind to it, it's easy to walk into situations and take control, or walk into a room and be the loudest voice—you just act with no restraint. It's easy to state your opinions and let your thoughts be known. It's a lot harder to choose not to lead when you feel you could—when you can be in charge, but you choose to let the one who *needs* to lead take charge in that moment for the better of your marriage or the situation at hand.

True power does not come from the raging river, but from the dam that harnesses its energy. It is a bridled tongue, not overflowing with words, but using them purposefully. Meekness and humility are power under control. A strong woman supporting her husband and laying down her life for her children—knowing full well she could dominate in any arena but having chosen instead to pour her heart and resources into where she is most needed as she equips those around her—to me, that is beauty and strength.

However, true strength isn't only found in the form of a stay-at-home mom. Many women don't have a choice in the matter and are needed to carry the weight of the financial burdens in the family. Many others simply choose to do so. There are women in positions of leadership in the working world, doing incredible things to improve the lives of those around them.

While all of this is fact, I'm simply asking you to rethink what strength actually is. Does strength only come from a domineering personality or from being outspoken? Can you be a rock for your people while on your knees in deep prayer? Can you be a pillar of strength by exuding patience and long-suffering to your toddlers? Can strength mean giving oneself to others, or does it come only to those who "get what they want"?

Perhaps our culture's definition of what a woman should be is misleading. We need to be prayerful about what each of us puts on our plate to leave a lasting impact on this generation and the one to come.

Ever since I was a little girl growing up in South Africa, it was my dream to be a singer and songwriter. At age 17, I signed a contract with an American record label. I was given the opportunity to be the front woman of a rock band, and after I finished school, we in the band moved overseas to pursue our dream.

Young love—our first tour

When I was 21, I met Jeremy on tour. It was evident the Lord's hand was on him. As our relationship developed, I knew my season of performing music was shifting, and I wanted to support him instead. A lot of people gave me a hard time for "squandering and wasting my gifting" and "taking a back seat," but in that season, after a lot of prayer, I chose to put my talents aside and pour into my husband and children. I still recorded two solo albums on the side and ran

a small boutique for a couple years, but my heart, soul, and strength were spent on my role as a stay-at-home mom.

We now have two teenagers with only a few more years left at home, and the daily demands of raising little ones have subsided. As time has flown by, you might think I've been tempted to resent the choice I made to put my

family before my career, but I have no regrets. I have had so many different opportunities to serve God with different talents; by no means has any time been wasted. If anything, I am thankful for all I have learned over the years, and I recognize every season of maturation has equipped me for what is

Welcoming Arie

to come. As doors open on various levels, I can wholeheartedly step through them, knowing I have poured into my family what I needed to in each season. Everything meaningful has a cost.

Don't be shortsighted in life. You can pursue dreams and raise a family. But don't be impatient and expect those things to happen all at once. Seek God's will for your life, and He will help you reach your full potential in every moment *and* in due time. And He will guide you through each season.

"A wise woman builds her home, but a foolish woman tears it down with her own hands" (Proverbs 14:1 NLT). How many times have you and I found this to be true of us? Sometimes we can be both the wise and the foolish all in one day. I pray the Lord will guide us and give us the strength to be all we need to be for those around us…to seek His will for our lives and not our own…to not be defined by our culture, but defined by Him.

We are his
workmanship, created
in Christ Jesus for
good works, which
God prepared
beforehand, that we
should walk in them.

EPHESIANS 2:10

— Jeremy's Journal —

Some men, when they hear the words "strong woman," have a preconceived notion of what that means. They think that she is domineering, strong-willed, rebellious, maybe overbearing, but they probably don't think of traits with a positive connotation.

Let me be transparent: When I was single, the thought of marrying a "strong woman" was not my idea of a fairy-tale relationship. My ideal was loving my quiet little wife, cherishing her with all my heart, and serving her as unselfishly as I knew how. I imagined coming home to a spotless house in perfect order. She would be dressed to the nines, awaiting me and excited to see her amazing husband when he came home. And in conflict, she would humbly understand my side at all times.

The first time Adrienne and I argued—and she definitely didn't see things my way—I was in for a rude awakening. Although my single self would never have dreamed of it, Adrienne's strength ended up being what I needed the most, and I realize now it's what I want the most. I love having someone who is strong enough to deal with this very selfish individual—me. The rubs we have are making me into a better man, even if I don't always see it at the time.

I also have a very strong personality, and when Adrienne and I are in situations where we may clash—if we are not under the submission of the Holy Spirit—our arguments could lead to a World War III–like explosion. On the other hand, the two of us together can become the fiercest warriors walking arm in arm, ready to serve the Lord unabashedly and wholeheartedly. Now, don't get me wrong—when we are acting in our flesh, even the mightiest fighters wouldn't want to get between us. We have really had to learn what it means to die to ourselves and fight *for* each other, instead of against.

I really love my wife—her passion, creativity, opinions, and insight. These are all such beautiful strengths, but they have brought challenges for me as well. There have been many times when I just wanted to come in and make decisions because I thought I had it all figured out already, and I didn't want her to question me. (Just to make it clear, I'm fully aware that I don't have it all figured out; but there are moments, if we're honest, when we all think we do.)

I would love to flow through life without the hiccups of differing opinions, but her questioning and, at times, pushback have made me the man I am today. Her insight has sharpened me and forced me to press into the Lord more for His direction. I have a tendency to jump headfirst into decisions, while Adrienne has more restraint, but we balance each other out. I'm a better person because of my wife and her strength.

There is nothing wrong with women who lead, as long as it's not at the expense of men failing in leadership. Men and women both need to step up and fulfill what God has for us. Our strengths should encourage and spur each other on.

God knows exactly what each of us needs. We may think we know, but He is omniscient, knowing everything. For this reason, I would rather trust His judgment than my own. If Adrienne didn't have the personality, strength, and ability to lead that she has been blessed with, then there is no way I would be able to do what I do. I travel continually, while she is incredible at holding down the fort at home, constantly pouring into our kids and being a support to me. Don't get me wrong—there are many times she is exhausted and at her wits' end. But I've never seen anyone put up with and deal with all she has had to endure. She works hard and juggles so much.

Let your spouse be who God made her to be, tempered and led by the Spirit, and you will see the dynamic change in your marriage for the better.

He who finds a wife finds a good thing and obtains favor from the LORD.

PROVERBS 18:22

In the same way husbands should love their wives as their own bodies. He who loves his wife loves himself.

EPHESIANS 5:28

You made all the delicate, inner parts of my body

and knit me together in my mother's womb.

Thank you for making me so wonderfully complex!

Your workmanship is marvelous—how well I know it.

You watched me as I was being formed

in utter seclusion,

as I was woven together in the dark of the womb.

You saw me before I was born.

Every day of my life was recorded in your book.

Every moment was laid out

before a single day had passed.

How precious are your thoughts about me, O God.

They cannot be numbered!

I can't even count them;

they outnumber the grains of sand!

And when I wake up,

you are still with me!

PSALM 139:13-18 NLT

Father God, help us have a fresh revelation of the depth of love You have for us. Help us delight ourselves in You first and foremost. Forgive us for looking to fleshly things to fulfill us and meet our needs when You are the only One who can truly accomplish that. Help us walk in humility, grow in maturity, and not be spiritual babies, but instead be rooted and established in You. Thank You for Your unfailing love. Amen.

Always be humble and gentle. Be patient with each other, making allowance for each other's faults because of your love. Make every effort to keep yourselves united in the Spirit, binding yourselves together with peace.

EPHESIANS 4:2-3 NLT

Is there any encouragement from belonging to Christ? Any comfort from his love? Any fellowship together in the Spirit? Are your hearts tender and compassionate? Then make me truly happy by agreeing wholeheartedly with each other, loving one another, and working together with one mind and purpose.

PHILIPPIANS 2:1-2 NLT

To keep your marriage brimming,
With love in the loving cup,
Whenever you're wrong, admit it;
Whenever you're right, shut up.

OGDEN NASH[1]

OUT OF ORDER

Jeremy once told me he can tell when I haven't been spending as much time with the Lord because I start to desire earthly things. In other words, I start looking to him to fulfill me. I might get a little more nitpicky, or perhaps I want him to pay more attention to me.

Of course, having your loved one pay attention to you is not a bad thing in general; it's when you start to demand it or rely upon it, or when you get particular about how it comes to you, that you have a problem.

"He's not loving me the way I want him to love me."

"She's not handling that the way I want her to handle it."

When you rely on your spouse to meet all your spiritual or emotional needs, you will only find yourself coming up short. It's like filling a bucket with a hole in it. We were never meant to be fully responsible for each other's emotional well-being. Consider marriage the "cherry on top." Jesus is the appetizer, main course, and dessert. Marriage is the chocolate sauce on your ice cream. It's impossible to have a healthy marriage without Jesus in the center of it all.

You cannot constantly look to your spouse to affirm you or to fill the recesses in your heart; you have to know your worth in Christ first. Right relationship with God produces right relationship with each other. Perhaps you notice yourself being controlling, fearful, or plagued by worry. Or maybe you're the one constantly covering up and propping up irresponsibleness, immaturity, or even addictions. All these behaviors will bring about an imbalance in your relationship, and it will be like trying to console a desperately hungry baby who is never satisfied. You or your spouse will have to feed and nurse your relationship constantly to keep the other person happy. You will be exhausted, and your marriage will be slow to mature.

Be committed to growing up with each other. Have honest and raw conversations about how to change these things, how to meet in the middle, how you can die to your flesh. Bring Jesus into the midst of it.

Don't be ashamed of counseling or marriage conferences. We all need tools to help us grow and change. Many of us come from dysfunctional families or carry baggage into our relationship with us. There are tools to be picked up from people who have gone before us. Please don't wait to ask for help until you've already decided it's the end. Take heed of your own heart.

Your union is worth the cost, even when it hurts. Good things are worth sacrifice.

I remember during one of our first arguments, we hit a wall. It dawned on me that we could both do something better, so I pitched my idea to Jeremy. "How about I work on being more intentional to not interrupt you while you're talking, if you can work on not accusing me?" It seemed a fair deal. A good compromise. That was the beginning of our learning to break bad habits by starting with a fairly simple step.

There have been many days when much more complicated conflicts have arisen, and the only compromise either of us could make was absolute surrender of everything to the Lord. I had to learn not to fight, but to trust the Lord to be my defense and pray that He would speak to my husband's heart—knowing full well that when a word comes from the Lord, it's a thousand times more effective than when it comes from me.

> The goal in marriage is not to think alike, but to think together.
>
> ROBERT C. DODDS[2]

WHERE DOES MY HELP COME FROM?

I was once really struggling with the weight of making sure Adrienne and the kids were okay—especially when it came to juggling the comings and goings of our life. Even though I was being intentional about asking them if they were all right, and they all responded with confidence, the enemy whispered that perhaps they were just trying to make me feel better and were too afraid to tell me the truth. Adrienne could see the weight and stress of all I was carrying, and one day she said to me, "Babe, as much as I love you and as much as you're my best friend, I don't need you as much as you think I do. I look to the Lord first, and He gives me what I need. Not that I don't also need you, but not like you think I do."

I was so relieved. Her trust in and dependence on God didn't give me the excuse to be withdrawn or absent, but it immediately brought a new freedom to our marriage, allowing me to love and encourage my family more.

I'm so thankful to have a wife who looks to the Lord and isn't constantly looking to me to fulfill every one of her needs. It makes me feel as if I can trust her with confidence. It diminishes the thought that I will never add up because, even on my best days, I know I will never be able to provide in every area for my family the way God does. I will give my all, but God is the only One who brings true peace and fulfillment.

I lift up my eyes to the hills.
From where does my help come?
My help comes from the LORD,
who made heaven and earth.

PSALM 121:1-2

All of you, clothe yourselves with
humility toward one another, because,
"God opposes the proud, but gives grace to
the humble." Humble yourselves, therefore,
under God's mighty hand, so that in due
time He may exalt you. Cast all your
anxiety on Him, because He cares for you.

1 PETER 5:5-7 BSB

— Adrienne's Journal —

I made my marriage vows on December 15, 2003. Although I was standing before Jeremy, my vow was to the Lord. I have often reminded him of that. My commitment to him is, in actuality, a commitment to the Lord first. Therefore, my loyalty and love for him are not based on how well he's performing as a husband.

Obviously, it is incredible when he is easy and wonderful to live with, but in all honesty, how often do husbands and wives operate on their best behavior with each other? Unfortunately, our spouses often get our leftovers. Because Jeremy's work is so varied, creative, and busy, he constantly has to deal with all kinds of people in many different ways; he is often exhausted. If I always looked to him for everything I desired, I would be sorely disappointed by his inability to fill my heart.

We are incapable of completely fulfilling each other. But since the vow I made was to Jesus, He never disappoints me when I look to Him. He is my safest place. He is always there in fullness. I delight myself in Him first, and Jeremy gets to benefit from the overflow of my relationship with Jesus.

DESIRING GOD MORE THAN EACH OTHER

How much love we have for Jesus will impact how much love we have for each other. When we delight ourselves in Him, our hearts are filled with His supernatural love. Our goal should be to have our own intimate, personal relationship with Jesus and to allow Him to help us become the right person, rather than expecting our spouse to be the perfect one for us.

There is no perfect person; you simply have sinners to choose from. But the Holy Spirit will be your teacher and lead you into truth. He will sustain you and help you learn how to deal with your significant other's flaws and weaknesses.

As much as Jeremy and I have already learned, and as hard as we are still working to communicate with each other, conflict remains. Through conflict we have had to look at ourselves with true humility and become more aware of our need for individual growth, as well as discover the way each of us clicks.

If you learn to deal with conflict the right way, you'll be much closer afterward.

9

THIS IS US

A good marriage is one where each partner secretly suspects they got the better deal.

UNKNOWN

Adrienne and I committed early on in our relationship to have knowing Jesus and making Him known be the driving force behind what we do and who we are. There wasn't a defining moment when we sat down and decided this, but through a series of conversations, we knew it was how we wanted to live our life. This commitment and vision for our life together brought in a sense of unspoken nonnegotiables, which included anything that would go against the biblical nature of the One we are following.

It's very important to have a vision for your marriage and your family.

WHY IS VISION IMPORTANT?

Consider this list, adapted from a post by Chantal Bechervaise:

- Vision shows you where you are headed.
- Vision motivates and inspires you to keep going.
- Vision keeps you moving forward through obstacles and difficulties.
- Vision provides focus and clarity.
- Vision gives meaning and purpose to what you do.[1]

Proverbs 29:18 says, "Where there is no vision, the people cast off restraint; but blessed is he who keeps the law" (BSB). This verse is actually talking about the revealed Word of God to His people or His divine communication to them. A lack of interaction with the Lord leaves people lost and, in a sense, wandering aimlessly.

The same is true for your marriage and family. You need God's wisdom for your life. Sometimes the Holy Spirit will highlight something in Scripture that will be a theme for a time or will act as a beacon for you through various seasons. It is important to know where you are headed in your marriage and to follow the Lord's wisdom and guidance.

> *By this all people will know that you are my disciples, if you have love for one another.*
>
> JOHN 13:35

Adrienne and I take time to sit down together with our children to talk about our vision for upcoming matters. We will even discuss various social and spiritual issues and what our views and beliefs about them are.

We believe our kids need to see faith modeled and lived out in front of them. That faith should be evident in the way we treat each other privately and interact with people publicly. The love we have should infiltrate all areas of our lives.

Faith is not just about checking off the to-do list of reading your Bible or going to church but about actually letting the truths of Scripture be active in your life. Your relationship with Jesus should spill over into all of who you are as you live and serve people around you, not just be a religious piece of your life's pie. No area should go untouched by the transforming love of Jesus. Of course, none of us have attained this, but it needs to be our desire to become more and more like Jesus as we venture through this life.

We long for our family to know His love and operate in it. Because of that, we have been intentional about what we allow our kids to be exposed to. We made a decision, as much as it's in our power, to limit—if not entirely prevent—our kids being exposed to certain influences of the world we feel would corrupt their thoughts, especially in the foundational years. This allows us to make sure we, not the world, are the ones who provide the narrative on certain important topics.

We want to establish a godly belief system for them first, before the world can have the chance to throw its own views at them. We want to teach our kids who God is and who He made them to be. We want to dive into Scripture together and let it be the guideline for how we live our lives and how we serve the Lord together. We want our children to have an eternal perspective on life issues and understand that, as believers, "our citizenship is in heaven" (Philippians 3:20), and this temporary world is not our home. We don't believe in hiding our kids away from the world but in giving them a biblical foundation on all issues in life, so they are rooted in the truth and, in turn, can be a light to those around them.

We believe in loving others around us, even when they have different belief systems or worldviews. There is no value in arguing with or bashing people in cowardly online rants, but there is much value in living lives that hopefully reflect the love and good news of Christ. He saved us and transformed our lives.

Our entire family has befriended and interacts with people who differ from us culturally, religiously, and spiritually on a regular basis. We have many discussions on why we believe what we do. We have told our children that no question is off limits. If what we believe isn't strong enough to stand after being tested or questioned, perhaps we need to dig a bit deeper and have a better understanding of our own belief systems in order to adequately pass them on and stimulate those around us.

You are witnesses, as is God himself, that our life among you believers was honest, straightforward and above criticism. You will remember how we dealt with each one of you personally, like a father with his own children, stimulating your faith and courage and giving you instruction. Our only object was to help you to live lives worthy of the God who has called you to share the splendour of his kingdom.

1 THESSALONIANS 2:10-12 PHILLIPS

SEEKING TRUTH

There was a season when our oldest daughter, Bella, questioned God's existence and whether or not she could hear His voice. She felt as though He were far away from her and was unsure if her prayers were being heard by Him, because she didn't seem to get the answers she desired. Adrienne talked about these doubts at length with her and told her it didn't worry or rattle us that she was questioning. The two of them studied some incredible apologetic resources together and prayed for God to reveal Himself to Bella. We expressed full confidence in the evidence of God's existence and in His character, which we have often discussed as a family—but it was important for her to come to those conclusions herself. And she did.

Understanding wasn't an overnight thing. In fact, there was about a year or so when Bella struggled from time to time, but after praying and studying different worldviews, she decided that even though she doesn't always feel God's nearness, the Christian worldview is by far the most cohesive. It hasn't

all been a mental decision for her either; there have been beautiful times during worship and reading her Bible when she has felt the Lord's presence.

We want our children to feel safe to ask the questions they have, so we can come alongside them and help direct them to the truth of God's Word. We want them to find out for themselves that He is constant and unchanging, even if their emotions are all over the place and certain prayers don't seem to be answered.

Bella and Arie's baptism

Every generation must do its own seeking and its own finding. The fault of the fathers often is that they expect their finding to stand in place of their children's seeking—expect the children to receive that which has satisfied the need of their fathers upon their testimony; whereas rightly, their testimony is not ground for their children's belief, only for their children's search. That search is faith in the bud.

GEORGE MACDONALD[2]

> The Bible doesn't say God will answer all prayers in the way we hope. We can't always know WHY it isn't God's will to grant a given prayer request, but we can be confident that God will answer in the way that is best in view of eternity.
>
> NATASHA CRAIN[3]

Our kids are fully familiar with this paradox because of my testimony. The Lord chose to heal my first wife, Melissa, on heaven's side of the veil and not here, as I was desperately believing and begging Him to do. Had He healed her, Adrienne and my three beautiful kids—whom I couldn't imagine life without—wouldn't be here with me. As hard as it was to walk through such devastating grief, I can see His hand in it all and how He has used my testimony to reach hundreds of thousands of people and bring hope.

You will seek me and find me,
when you seek me with all your heart.

JEREMIAH 29:13

All truth is given by revelation,
either general or special, and it must
be received by reason. Reason is the
God-given means for discovering the
truth that God discloses, whether in
his world or his Word. While God
wants to reach the heart with truth,
he does not bypass the mind.

JONATHAN EDWARDS[4]

ON MISSION TOGETHER

When the girls were really young, we wanted to teach them to practice hiding God's Word in their hearts. A passage of Scripture from Romans stood out as one we should memorize together. It subsequently became somewhat

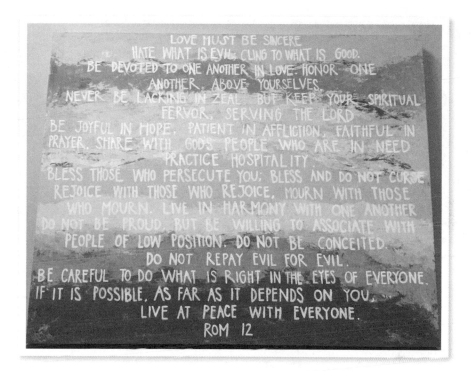

of a motto for our family, and we have referenced it many times on our journey of life together. Adrienne wrote it on our bathroom mirror for a while, and since then she has painted it on a huge wooden canvas that stands in the corner of our bedroom:

> Love must be sincere. Hate what is evil; cling to what is good. Be devoted to one another in love. Honor one another above yourselves. Never be lacking in zeal, but keep your spiritual fervor, serving the Lord. Be joyful in hope, patient in affliction, faithful in prayer. Share with the Lord's people who are in need. Practice hospitality.

Fun Fact

When I was little girl, we had a decent-sized backyard, where we would spend countless hours playing. Instead of yelling to get our attention, my mom would ring a cowbell to call us inside. I have since adopted a similar custom: I ring a bell for meals only. It's amazing to see the kids instantly scurry into the kitchen. I will definitely miss that sight one day when we are empty nesters.

Bless those who persecute you; bless and do not curse. Rejoice with those who rejoice; mourn with those who mourn. Live in harmony with one another. Do not be proud, but be willing to associate with people of low position. Do not be conceited.

Do not repay anyone evil for evil. Be careful to do what is right in the eyes of everyone. If it is possible, as far as it depends on you, live at peace with everyone. Do not take revenge, my dear friends, but leave room for God's wrath, for it is written: "It is mine to avenge; I will repay," says the Lord. On the contrary:

> "If your enemy is hungry, feed him;
> if he is thirsty, give him something to drink.
> In doing this, you will heap burning coals on his head."

> Do not be overcome by evil, but overcome evil with good
> (Romans 12:9-21 NIV).

Although we started out with the goal of simply memorizing Scripture, this passage has become a huge part of the direction we have taken as a family, instilling God's culture into our lives.

"SOCIAL REBELLION" AS A FAMILY STRATEGY

As a family who travels and does ministry together, we have taken our children into a wide variety of circumstances. They have been in many different countries—in the wealthiest of places with high-profile people and in the most run-down, sometimes-disease-impacted places with people barely clothed.

There have been many times when we've rubbed shoulders or befriended people who don't necessarily see eye to eye with our family on everything, as you may have experienced yourself. Many people have their own customs and ways of dealing with life that may seem peculiar to you. Perhaps they believe in the rapture; perhaps they don't. Perhaps they drink alcohol; perhaps they don't. Perhaps their kids are allowed to participate in activities you have decided would be best for your children to avoid. Perhaps they listen to secular music and watch screens all day. Perhaps they eat only organic, non-GMO foods. Perhaps they allow their kids to talk back and argue. The list of the unique characteristics found in each family could go on and on. All the while, these differing families profess to love Jesus, however their day-to-day family culture might contrast with yours.

> *Always be humble and gentle. Be patient with each other, making allowance for each other's faults because of your love.*
>
> EPHESIANS 4:2 NLT

As much as certain measures of protection might be necessary, you can't hide under a rock forever. How do we live alongside people with diverse family cultures and yet stay true to who our family is as we grow in maturity and pursue a closer walk with Jesus?

Before we enter various out-of-the-norm scenarios, we will often have a family pep talk. We try to address what we can expect from the situation, the people we may encounter, and how we as a family want to be perceived. It's an opportunity to reemphasize what we believe as a family. No matter what may be going on around us, we know we are in it together—and above all else that happens, we want to love people around us authentically. Jesus interacted with sinners and people who were very different from Him, but He never became like them. Instead, He brought the change to them. In the same way, we have committed as a family to be influencers to those around us.

We know who we are in Christ because we talk about it and seek Him together. We want to live in a way that makes a difference to those around us, as our belief in God should impact our lives on a daily basis. As Jesus says in Matthew 5:14-16, "You are the light of the world. A city that is set on a hill cannot be hidden. Nor do they light a lamp and put it under a basket, but on a lampstand, and it gives light to all who are in the house. Let your light so shine before men, that they may see your good works and glorify your Father in heaven" (NKJV).

PRAYER

Lord Jesus, please give us a fresh revelation of who You are. Help us love others the way You love them. May Your countenance shine on us and help us influence and encourage those around us to pursue You more. Help us be steadfast and immovable in our faith as we walk alongside those who are different from us, that we would bear with one another patiently and in love, just as You constantly do with us. Thank You for Your grace and mercy in our lives. Amen.

The life of Jesus in us was never meant to be hidden from others but instead to bring light and truth to those around us.

We're to encourage each other and build each other up in love. Each one of us could handle a greater measure of walking in love toward those around us, no matter where they may be spiritually. As we encounter Jesus and find more and more fulfillment in Him, we will lead others to find Him as they see the evidence of His work in our lives.

After the disciples came face to face with the resurrected Jesus, they were radically transformed from once cowardly deserting Him to being filled with such boldness that thousands of people chose to believe based on their testimony. They went from hiding and denying their discipleship to risking their lives to share what Jesus had done for them.

Perhaps at times we may feel like Peter, who denied his affiliation with Jesus, or like John, who followed and watched Jesus' trial from a distance. But I pray we would ask the Lord to help us encounter Him afresh, that our hearts would be filled with an unquenchable love for Him and boldness to share the hope of what He has done in our lives with others around us.

Ebenezer Stones

The word *ebenezer* actually comes from 1 Samuel 7.

God's people, the Israelites, had wandered away from Him and were worshipping idols. The prophet and judge, Samuel, challenged them: "If you are returning to the Lord with all your heart, then put away the foreign gods and the Ashtaroth from among you and direct your heart to the Lord and serve him only, and he will deliver you out of the hand of the Philistines" (verse 3). They had a radical change of heart that day, confessed their sins, and got rid of their foreign gods. While they were repenting, the Philistines gathered their armies to attack. (Doesn't that sound exactly like the enemy when we're in a season of breakthrough?)

The Israelites became deeply fearful and begged Samuel not to stop pleading to God on their behalf.

Verse 10 tells us, "Just as Samuel was sacrificing the burnt offering, the Philistines arrived to attack Israel. But the Lord spoke with a mighty voice of thunder from heaven that day, and the Philistines were thrown into such confusion that the Israelites defeated them" (NLT).

The Lord intervened, heard their cries for help, and gave them victory. And Samuel placed a large stone in their midst and called it "Ebenezer," which means "stone of help," as a reminder of what the Lord had done for them (verse 12 NLT). Whenever they would see it, they would remember the battle the Lord had fought on their behalf. It was a tangible reminder of God's power and protection over them.

As we continue through the daily grind of life, it's important for us to stop and create tangible reminders of what God has done for us—not only to share how He saved us with those around us, but to share what He does for us on a regular basis. How can we acknowledge God in our daily lives but not get so familiar with His grace that we forget the height from which we once fell? When we stop to thank Him for what He does in our lives, we cultivate a culture of remembrance and gratitude to the One who holds all things together.

Only be on your guard and diligently watch yourselves, so that you do not forget the things your eyes have seen, and so that they do not slip from your heart as long as you live. Teach them to your children and grandchildren.

DEUTERONOMY 4:9 BSB

Leave and Cleave

Years ago, Jeremy's mom and I had a phone conversation about the importance of creating traditions within our own homes and not just following the habits of the family into which we married. We talked about how sweet it is to have familiarity with our immediate family, so when the patriarchs or matriarchs pass away, we have traditions we have made our own.

Perhaps your family's traditions resemble what your extended families have always done, or perhaps they are completely unique. As you create your own family traditions, begin by talking through which traditions in each of your families are worth keeping and which ones no longer need to be followed. Be willing to "leave and cleave" (Genesis 2:24) and create your own family culture.

One of the ways we have put this into practice is by taking each Christmas as it comes. This might make traditionalists freak out, but we love it. There are things we do the same every year, such as sitting down as a family and reading Luke 2 before we open our gifts, but some years look completely different from all others. Sometimes we have a special brunch, other times a special dinner—and the menu is always up for discussion. We ask ourselves, *What's the best for our family this year?*

Because of the way our family is boomeranged away and back all year long, we sit down each holiday season and talk about what will bring the

most peace to us. We make our decision based on the tight circle of our family alone. Although we would love to please everyone and be in numerous places at one time, we have to look for what breathes life into our immediate family. You should still honor extended family, but remember that you're building something new—and hopefully your kids will do the same when they have their own spouses and children.

10

I CAN'T DO THIS ANYMORE

If we're honest, most strife in marriage comes from sin. Petty arguments may arise from selfishness, jealousy, or bitterness, while serious problems may be sourced from addiction, adultery, or lying. When marriage "stinks," what should we do?

IS THERE ANY HOPE?

When I was a young teenager, I read a book called, *What's So Amazing About Grace?* by Philip Yancey. It made an impact on me in that season of my life and made me think through what kind of person I was going to be to those around me. Yancey talked about how we can have a tendency to operate in cycles of "ungrace" toward each other. As people who have received so much grace and mercy from the Lord, we should instead rush to forgive each other and restore relationship.

In our days as newlyweds, I remember being in the middle of an argument with Jeremy. He was on the road, so we had our argument over the phone. He hastily hung up in one of those *I'm done talking about this! Click!* moments. I despise conversations ending like that, and I was frustrated with him. But the break in conversation served us well. I immediately drew myself to the Lord in prayer. And He reminded me of what I had read years before about being the one to break the cycle of "ungrace." Even though Jeremy had started the argument, I had most certainly contributed to it and knew I had to own my part. No excuses. I called him back, apologized, and took responsibility for my wrongdoing.

At the end of the day, I have to answer to the Holy Spirit, and I was fully aware at that time that He was highlighting things in my attitude that were not right. Needless to say, my apology softened Jeremy's heart, and the argument came to a screeching halt.

Since God chose you to be the holy people he loves, you must clothe yourselves with tenderhearted mercy, kindness, humility, gentleness, and patience. Make allowance for each other's faults, and forgive anyone who offends you. Remember, the Lord forgave you, so you must forgive others. Above all, clothe yourselves with love, which binds us all together in perfect harmony. And let the peace that comes from Christ rule in your hearts. For as members of one body you are called to live in peace.

COLOSSIANS 3:12-15 NLT

> A soft answer turns away wrath,
> but a harsh word stirs up anger.
> The tongue of the wise uses
> knowledge rightly,
> but the mouth of fools pours
> forth foolishness.
>
> PROVERBS 15:1-2 NKJV

I committed in my heart to be the one to say, "I'm sorry," as quickly as I could. It definitely diffused and ended a lot of contentions. But after years went by, my motives turned prideful, and I found myself becoming bitter about always being the first one to apologize. I started thinking things like, *I'm tired of being the one to apologize first!* and, *I'm definitely not apologizing this time. He's been a total jerk—it's his turn to make this right.*

At one point I even dared to voice this feeling to Jeremy; it just added fuel to the fire. Although my jab made him think, I could have been transparent about my feelings in a completely different way and without any residual damage. The Holy Spirit very quickly pricked my heart, asking me if I was laying my rights down for Him or Jeremy. Whether or not Jeremy should have been apologizing first was irrelevant. I could trust the Lord as I humbled myself before Him; He would be my shield and defense.

Yes, even when it *really* hurts, I can be a peacemaker and trust God to right any wrongs done or said. As we tell our kids on a regular basis, "Two wrongs don't make a right."

> Fear not, for I am with you;
> be not dismayed, for I am your God;
> I will strengthen you, I will help you,
> I will uphold you with my righteous
> right hand.
>
> ISAIAH 41:10

I know Jeremy has a relationship with the Lord, and I have had to learn to trust God to be the one to soften and speak to his heart. In our early days of marriage, Jeremy was slow to own his side and apologize; as we have grown together in this, he often beats me to it. I have also learned a genuine apology has no self-righteousness or strings attached.

> *Hatred stirs up strife,*
> *but love covers all sins.*
>
> PROVERBS 10:12 NKJV

Even though I approached resolving our arguments with a right attitude initially, the longer we were together, the more I started carrying an offense against Jeremy for his lack. I started keeping score in my heart of what he had done wrong. I felt indifferent toward him because of the hurt I felt. I knew I needed to change if I didn't want my heart to become hardened.

Sometimes we read Scripture or hear a message or a song and know that it's meant for us, but it just doesn't seem to penetrate our walled-off hearts. I knew God was showing me how to change my circumstances, and yet I couldn't seem to make His nudging have an effect on me. I couldn't manufacture a heart-softening response. I wanted to break but just couldn't. I felt numb.

Have there been times when you have felt frustrated beyond what you can bear? All you can do is stand by as pain ambushes your heart and cuts to the deepest parts. Or perhaps your feet are stuck in what feels like the thickest concrete, impenetrable to the world's strongest jackhammer. No matter what you do, you still find yourself up against the same old grievances. You have no love left; you feel calloused, if you even feel anything at all. Maybe the nothingness has already turned to hatred in your heart.

In Mark 5, Jesus was begged by one of the local rulers to come and heal his dying daughter. Jesus, seemingly in no hurry at all, makes His way to the ruler's home. He apparently misses His appointment, and the family friends tell the ruler not to bother Jesus because the girl has already died. However, when Jesus hears these words, His response is, "Do not be afraid; only believe" (verse 36 NKJV).

Jesus still visits the house, even when it seems hopeless. And the crowd makes fun of Him, perhaps saying things like, "Oh, please. What's left here? There's no hope. She has no heartbeat. They tried everything. Who does Jesus think He is, anyway?"

But Jesus puts the noisy, unbelieving crowd outside—completely away—and takes the parents into a quiet place, shutting the door behind them. He walks over to the little girl and commands her to arise. She instantly gets off her deathbed and lives! Jesus then tells them to feed and nourish her frail frame.

Is this little girl your heart or marriage? Have you begged Jesus for healing, and yet He seems slow to respond? Is the crowd noisy and constantly cluttering your mind with unbelief? Whatever despondency or even death you feel in your situation, put the negative, unbelieving crowd *away*, whatever that might mean for you. Put away your own negative thoughts and feelings, the influence of parents or family members with strong opinions, the words of friends who are not filled with faith in the victory of your marriage. Divorce the idea of divorce. We make too many exceptions for it in our day.

Then, with an open and willing heart, bring yourself into a quiet place with Jesus and make yourself available for a healing touch from Him. Shut the door on everything else and quiet your heart before Him. Let Him breathe His life back into your heart. Let Him be the One to silence the mocking crowd and speak, "Arise," into the fibers of your love for each other.

Then get up. Get off your sickbed and go feed your marriage with something healthy. Renew your mind with Scripture and prayer. No matter how many times you need to come back to this place of asking Jesus to speak His resurrection into your heart, don't let the noisiness of life stop you. Cry out to Him for what you need.

Unfortunately, the sickness of our flesh is not cured in one day, but by repeatedly coming to the Lord and asking Him to transform us, He changes us into the likeness of His son.

> All of us who have had that veil removed can see and reflect the glory of the Lord. And the Lord—who is the Spirit—makes us more and more like him as we are changed into his glorious image.
>
> 2 CORINTHIANS 3:18 NLT

WHEN YOU WANT TO WANDER

I'm not at all against romantic movies. Who isn't captivated by a wonderful, sweet story of love conquering and defying all odds? However, when we were in our earlier years of marriage, I watched a romantic comedy with some friends and was disturbed by the effect it had on my heart. I remember feeling disappointed in the lack of dreamy romance in my marriage. I wished that Jeremy were more in tune with my heart, that he would read my every thought and make me feel special. As days went by, I began to think through it all and realized the enemy was trying to plant a seed of dissatisfaction and discontentment in my heart.

Everything I was longing for was centered around how it made me *feel*. These new dreams were all based on my emotions, which can waver with every gust of wind. My thoughts were all self-serving. I realized that what I had seen on the big screen was a complete fantasy. Real love (not movie love) consists of lifelong companionship. It's two people walking through the ever-changing seasons of life together, along sometimes long and hard roads, hand in hand. Love is not idealistic perfection. It's more like your favorite pair of jeans that you put on over and over because they're comfortable, fit you well, and have been there for years. All joking aside, love should endure all things (1 Corinthians 13:7).

Marriage is not centered around a perfectly played-out romance. There is some of that, especially in the beginning, but a good marriage is built on an intimate friendship—knowing each other's ins and outs and still loving each other.

Perhaps you feel lured away or enamored by how special someone else makes you feel. That person finally treats you the way you want to be treated. But the grass is always greener on the other side—until you have to live life with that person, and you realize that your new flame is just as quirky as the person you were with before. Yes, even this one has the ability to annoy you and push your buttons. Perhaps their idiosyncrasies are different, but they are irritating, nevertheless.

Instead of looking for fulfillment outside your marriage, go to God first and make things right with Him. No human can ever satisfy or complete the longings in our hearts; only Jesus can fill us. Perhaps the very thing you feel you need is the very thing your spouse is terrible at giving. Does that grant you permission to look elsewhere? No. Go to the Lord, beg Him for what is lacking in your heart, and do everything you can to protect your marriage and keep your heart from wandering.

Give all your worries and cares to God, for he cares about you.

1 PETER 5:7 NLT

PORNOGRAPHY IS EVERYWHERE

True story: I had a Christian man once tell me that he subscribed to certain inappropriate magazines, featuring barely clothed women, because he enjoyed reading the articles. He completely justified his engagement with this sort of indulgence. Somewhere along the line, he bought into the lie that seeing just a little bit of skin on another woman was totally acceptable and never hurt anyone.

The enemy is not lacking in tactics to plant seeds of deception, and they almost always start small. It's a sad reality that the objectification of women is everywhere. It is almost impossible to hide from salacious images, but just because they're readily available does not give us an excuse to participate in viewing them.

I've heard it said for years, "It's not the first look, but the second and third and so on." When I was a young man, this statement seemed unrelatable and quite "churchy," but as I've gotten older, I've come to realize how true it is. You can genuinely intend to walk in total purity when an image is suddenly thrust in front of your face, and you have to make a decision: *What do I do with that?* Do you go back for just one more intriguing look, or do you turn away and literally beg the Lord to help you not struggle with the picture now in your mind—the picture you never asked for in the first place?

Listen, I know it's easier said than done in the moment, but it's important to understand that the enemy realizes our weaknesses and will piggyback on any opportunity to take us down. As we all know, when a soldier prepares for battle, that's exactly what he's doing: preparing for an inevitable fight.

The more prepared you are, the better chances you have at victory. This is where the battle is won—starting your day with your heart prepared and mind guarded. If you wait until the temptation arises to try and fight, then it will be a much more difficult struggle, and you're more likely to get knocked off your feet.

During a flight, I once watched a very sad movie with a disturbing ending. In *Million Dollar Baby*, a boxer who came from nothing fights to become one of the best and fiercest boxers around. Her trainer would tell her to always protect herself. In one moment of elation over the inevitable defeat of her opponent, a well-known dirty boxer, the heroine lets her guard down. As the bell rings, the other boxer takes a cheap shot to the back of her head, rendering her completely paralyzed. After this tragedy, as she lies strikingly still in her hospital room, she confesses that she hadn't protected herself.

I use this analogy because we have to realize the enemy does not abide by rules. He comes to steal, kill, and destroy (John 10:10), and his tactics won't always be obvious. He will come at you with every cheap shot you can imagine. Don't let your guard down. As the Bible says, "Take heed lest [you] fall" (1 Corinthians 10:12). The moment you think you are doing well or winning in an area, and you let your guard down or let yourself go unprotected—that's when the barrage of attacks from the enemy begins. And no one is exempt from his advances.

Aside from hiding God's Word in my heart, one of the ways I keep my guard up, especially when I travel without Adrienne, is by never putting myself in a situation alone with another woman. I have a friend or bandmate with me always.

Jesus challenges us to abide by a higher moral law in Matthew 5:28: "I say, anyone who even looks at a woman with lust has already committed adultery with her in his heart" (NLT). Don't go easy on yourself. Don't make excuses.

I have a handful of close friends, along with Adrienne, and we ask one another bold questions related to accountability and purity because we know that the damage pornography does to relationships is devastating. This is true for men and women alike. Pornography causes hardness in our hearts and makes us become detached emotionally and stunted spiritually.

> How can a young person stay
> on the path of purity?
> By living according to your word.
> I seek you with all my heart;
> do not let me stray from your commands.
> I have hidden your word in my heart
> that I might not sin against you.
>
> PSALM 119:9-11 NIV

> *I will not look with approval*
> *on anything that is vile.*
> *I hate what faithless people do;*
> *I will have no part in it.*
>
> PSALM 101:3 NIV

Pray for each other. Pray for protection over your marriage and against the wiles of the enemy. This is not just a struggle for men alone; women are just as much of a target. Pray your spouse will be convicted and exposed if he or she is ever drawn into looking at something lewd.

> *Be on your guard; stand firm in the faith;*
> *be courageous; be strong.*
>
> 1 CORINTHIANS 16:13 NIV

What If You've Really Blown It?

We feel highly unqualified to speak into this area; we can only share with you what we have learned along our own journey of marriage. We would implore couples to seek godly, biblical counseling to heal a broken marriage. Don't go at it alone. There are seasons when we need other people to walk closely alongside us. And don't give up: God can breathe life into the most damaged relationships.

If you have hurt or betrayed your spouse, don't dare to ask them, "Are you over it yet?" Come clean. Be humble, repent, and show remorse—however many times you need to do so. Be patient while your spouse heals. Trust takes time to be rebuilt.

If you have been hurt, be transparent about what you feel, but don't punish your spouse with a revengeful attitude, thinking, *Because you hurt me, I'll hurt you back...*

God wouldn't give us the command to forgive if He didn't know that He could equip us with supernatural forgiveness. Unforgiveness is like a swarm of termites wreaking havoc on the inner walls of your heart. You can't subdivide and tell it where to stay. It will eventually eat away at everything. Ask God to manifest His supernatural love in you.

NAKED AND UNASHAMED

The man and his wife were both naked and were not ashamed
(Genesis 2:25).

Oneness in marriage is something spiritual—it represents not only the unity of God's triune character, but also the love He has for His church. True intimacy comes from being fully known and loved, imperfections and all. Our physical union in marriage as two "become one flesh" (Genesis 2:24) should be deep, beautiful, and pure.

By bringing Hollywood fantasies into the bedroom and leaving Jesus out of it, sex has become idolized. The goal of sex in a marriage is mutual enjoyment. And there are other ways to fan the flames of physical intimacy than through the act of sex itself. Affectionate, nonsexual touches: stroking their hair, touching their back as you walk past. Caring conversations, openness, and honesty with each other. Having a time of prayer together. Paying attention to the details.

Your spouse is not just any spouse—they're *yours*.

We need to take time to listen to each other and grow together. Putting someone else's needs above your own builds trust. The more you're known, the safer you feel. The safer you feel, the freer you will be with each other. In order to have meaningful physical engagement, emotional engagement needs to be there. Although women are usually seen as the ones who need the most emotional connection, men absolutely need a place of safe connection as well.

Ask yourself: *What are the hindrances to intimacy in my marriage? Am I being trustworthy? Am I doing something that is unloving or causing my spouse to feel disrespected or torn down?*

And don't forget to have fun. Enjoy enjoying each other.

> *Let your fountain be blessed,*
> *and rejoice in the wife of your youth,*
> *a lovely deer, a graceful doe.*
> *Let her breasts fill you at*
> *all times with delight;*
> *be intoxicated always in her love.*
>
> PROVERBS 5:18-19

11

ENVISIONING
THE FUTURE

The saying "Hindsight is twenty-twenty" is popular—almost cliché—because it is true. When we look back on our lives and note how we've changed from when we were teenagers to where we are now, we see our mistakes, successes, and growth in ways we could not while we were living out those years. Time gives perspective and encourages reflection on our lives and relationships, including our marriages.

I vividly remember the day Jeremy and I got married. There was no human on the planet to whom I felt closer, but little did I know we were practically strangers on our wedding day. We had our personal habits and routines that would soon cause friction simply from us rubbing together in our daily interactions. At the end of many days, we'd each think the other had arrived from another planet altogether. Compared to how well we know each other now and the depth of friendship that exists between us, I realize the closeness I felt to Jeremy on our wedding day was only a shadow of what was to come. I look forward to growing closer over the years we will have together.

Couples start out wholeheartedly envisioning their life together in a certain way, full of plans and dreams. However, we have no idea what the future has in store for us or how each of us will handle the trials and temptations thrown our way. If we see our marriages as lifelong journeys in which we can grow and evolve, then I believe we will live each interval of life with a lot more grace and understanding.

What are we sowing into our marriages today to make them last the next fifty-plus years? None of us desire to be dull roommates, barely mumbling a few words to each other here and there. None of us are who we used to be or who we want to be, having attained every life goal or spiritual victory we desire. There will be hurt, heartache, and disappointments, as well as victories, triumphs, celebrations, and festivities. Each changing season will require adjustments and sacrifice. It's impossible to love deeply without these things.

It might take years for us to realize we can no longer live for ourselves and our own desires, but the sooner we leave behind our single lives and attitudes, habits and routines, and become intentional about forging our union, the sooner we will see the gratifying potentials of marriage.

This is how we know what love is:
Jesus Christ laid down his life for us.
And we ought to lay down our lives
for our brothers and sisters.

1 JOHN 3:16 NIV

What marriage is for: It is a way for
two spiritual friends to help each
other on their journey to become the
persons God designed them to be.

TIMOTHY KELLER[1]

THE WAY FORWARD

The only way to have a truly healthy marriage is to live in unison with Jesus. If we remain in Him, everything else in our lives will be permeated by the fullness of His life in us. If Jesus isn't the focus and center of our lives, then someone or something else is.

Jesus made the process for following Him very clear: deny ourselves, pick up our crosses, and follow Him (Luke 9:23). Obviously, it is impossible to literally follow Him to crucifixion every day, carrying a cross on our backs as Simon of Cyrene did (Luke 23:26), so what did Jesus mean by these three instructions?

In the Roman Empire, the cross was a preferred instrument of capital punishment, used to torture and kill the flesh. When the apostle Paul wrote

> He died for all, that those who live should no longer live for themselves but for him who died for them and was raised again.
>
> 2 CORINTHIANS 5:15 NIV

> *The only way to dispossess [the heart] of an old affection, is by the expulsive power of a new one.*
>
> THOMAS CHALMERS[2]

to the Galatians, he explained that the actions of the "flesh"—the "self" Jesus told us to deny—are any behaviors, intentions, or attitudes that go against the desires of the Spirit (Galatians 5:19-24). All that might sound a tad sadistic and scary, but it's important that we prayerfully quiet ourselves before the Lord, hit the refresh button on the browsers of our hearts, and surrender all we do to Him daily. When we know the goodness of the Lord and the fullness of life found in Him, those daily sacrifices of our will become a joy to us. As we deny ourselves and follow Him, the Spirit fills us with love, joy, peace, patience, kindness, goodness, faithfulness, gentleness, and self-control (verses 22-23).

We know that God's heart for His people is constant throughout the entirety of Scripture. We know from His unchanging character and the sacrifice of His Son that He loves us without conditions. He hasn't changed His mind about His feelings for us. We can trust that when He asks us to surrender our wants and wills to Him, it is for our best.

> Many, Lord my God,
> are the wonders you have done,
> the things you planned for us.
> None can compare with you;
> were I to speak and tell of your deeds,
> they would be too many to declare.
>
> PSALM 40:5 NIV

> The Lord, He is the One who goes before you. He will be with you, He will not leave you nor forsake you; do not fear nor be dismayed.
>
> DEUTERONOMY 31:8 NKJV

When we find our identities in Jesus, we are no longer bound or burdened by anything else. Being a slave to Christ paradoxically brings the greatest amount of freedom. As we lose ourselves in Him, we will find a deeper sense of reason and purpose.

Self-preoccupation, self-broodings, self-interest, self-love—these are the reasons why you go jarring against your fellows. Turn your eyes off yourself... Look up and out, from this narrow, cabined self of yours, and you will jar no longer, you will fret no more, you will provoke no more, you will quarrel no more; but you will, to your own glad surprise, find the secret of "the meekness and the gentleness of Jesus"...and the fruits of the spirit will all bud and blossom from out of your life.

HENRY SCOTT HOLLAND[3]

FORGIVENESS

We have a tradition with some of our best friends: We order takeout Indian food and play Catan for hours. We play on a foam game board etched with scribbled victories, memories, and favorite quotes from our evenings together. Jeremy definitely holds the record for the funniest quotes. One night he blurted out, "My pain is worse, because it's mine!" We all roared with laughter, and of course the line made it to the board.

But isn't that so often the case? Our pain feels worse to us because we're the ones feeling it. When someone does something to hurt us, we hold on to that pain, rehearse the stinging scene over and over in our heads, and nurse and feed it like we would a demanding newborn baby.

> Do not take to heart everything people say,
> lest you hear your servant cursing you.
> For many times, also, your own
> heart has known
> that even you have cursed others.
>
> ECCLESIASTES 7:21-22 NKJV

We can be easily offended by how others are acting, and yet we carry quiet, self-righteous pride. Do we give the grace to others that we ourselves expect? Do we forgive the way we want to be forgiven? Do we hold our spouse to a higher level than ourselves? There are times we may have hurt someone just as much as they have hurt us, so when we demand an apology, we should remember how much wrong we have done to others.

When the girls were younger, Jeremy's touring schedule was insanely busy. As often as we tried to travel together as a family, there were days and weeks I juggled life as a single mom. I often felt drained of pretty much all of my energy, and it seemed everyone expected something of me, even Jeremy. Then an opportunity arose for me to go out of town for a couple nights, and I gladly accepted, thinking Jeremy would finally have to watch the girls by himself and would get a solid dose of my daily exhaustion—hopefully gaining a greater understanding for how much I had on my plate. I imagined that when I got home, he would gush about how much he admired and appreciated all my labor.

Traveling with littles

Much to my dismay, when I called to check on how everyone was coping, I found out Jeremy had hired a babysitter and was having a jolly-good time with his friends.

I was livid. My plan had blown up in my face. The worst part of it was that I couldn't say anything to him because he didn't know about my ulterior motive of teaching him a lesson.

On another occasion, Jeremy was frustrated with me and complained that I never showered enough or went to much effort to look after myself. (Cue judging of every overworked woman everywhere.) One day, while I was gone for an afternoon, he cleaned and vacuumed the entire house to prove the point that there was enough time in the day to do it all. My feelings were so hurt when I arrived home. It was easy for Jeremy to step into "mom mode" for a day, but I was living there—day in and day out—carrying the weight while he was away. He, too, had the ulterior motive of teaching me a lesson; he was just less subtle about it.

We both learned the hard way that passive-aggressive lesson teaching is not being supportive of each other. It isn't the healthy way forward, and we weren't sowing anything positive or mature into our relationship. It only caused hurt because our hearts were not for each other in those moments. Each of us thought we had the heavier load and were trying to prove that point.

Every day, in every circumstance, we both have a weight to bear and value to bring. We both have to make sacrifices, and so we have had to learn to deal with each other in far more gracious ways. We all should spend more time thanking the Lord for our spouses than criticizing them.

> *Every time we forgive, we set a prisoner free, and the prisoner we set free is ourselves.*
>
> LEWIS B. SMEDES[4]

Forgiveness is the key which unlocks the door of resentment and the handcuffs of hatred. It breaks the chains of bitterness and the shackles of selfishness...Forgiveness is an act of the will, and the will can function regardless of the temperature of the heart.

CORRIE TEN BOOM[5]

Give me the love that leads the way,
The faith that nothing can dismay,
The hope no disappointments tire,
The passion that will burn like fire;
Let me not sink to be a clod:
Make me Thy fuel, Flame of God.

AMY CARMICHAEL[6]

LIFE AS A TEAM

I have a practice of setting aside special one-on-one times with my children. I take my girls on daddy-daughter dates, and Egan and I have "bro time." When Bella and Arie were younger, we would stretch out our arms as wide as we could and say, "I love you *this* much." Such a sweet, fun, connecting moment.

One day I took Bella out for ice cream. Everything we did that day paled in comparison to the thrill of knowing she was about to enjoy the sugar rush of a lifetime. When she received her treat, she thoroughly devoured the cone filled high with ice cream and held it as close to her chest as possible.

With my arms wide open, I looked at her and said in the most excited way possible, "I love you *thiiiiiiis* much." She looked at me, glanced at her ice cream, and held out only one arm as far as she could. She would not let that cone leave her chest as she responded with a somewhat wary, "I love you this much."

It struck me how many times we come to Jesus and do the same, saying, "I love you this much," without wanting to let go of our burdens.

> Now a certain man was there who had an infirmity thirty-eight years. When Jesus saw him lying there, and knew that he already had been in that condition a long time, He said to him, "Do you want to be made well?" (John 5:5-6 NKJV).

Jesus asked the man a direct question to cut to the core of his heart. How badly did he want healing?

God knows we get comfortable in our situations, even if they are unhealthy. Sometimes when we have been offended by our spouse, it might feel empowering to hold their misbehavior over them. We may place walls up to protect ourselves or find a way to retaliate. These unhealthy practices leave us crippled when we let them become commonplace in our lives.

The question is, do we want to be made well? Jesus is always willing to help us and take away our burdens, but we must be truly willing to surrender everything.

Loneliness and painful burdens can exist on both sides of your wedding vows, but when you and your spouse tackle life as a team, there is a sense of community and the reassurance of having someone in your corner. Either one of you may take a harder hit than the other at times, but no matter what comes in life, you have each other. Adrienne and I believe this indivisibility can only come when you're first and foremost connected with the Father. Out of the overflow of your relationship with Him, you will be able to walk in unison with each other.

It's important to have a clear vision of what you want for your family—to prioritize your family values and know what you stand for together. You can communicate and cultivate these things through many different activities, including mealtimes with no screens allowed, devotions and Scripture readings, and times of worship and prayer. Another way is to sit down and write a family mission statement.

If your family is anything like ours, then sitting down together for long, focused, thoughtful discussions is often difficult, as the kids can be easily distracted and fidgety. Even if it drives you nuts, press through and fight for these precious times together—they will be worth it in the end. You won't somehow arrive at your goals accidentally; you have to have a vision and mission to work your way there. You must be intentional as the Holy Spirit guides and leads your family to seek God together, and you must prayerfully reinforce what you believe is important. Talk through and discuss what each of you thinks those priorities should be.

Your family's mission statement doesn't have to be fancy. Here is an example:

We desire to…
keep our zeal and hunger for the Lord.
show love and honor to those around us.
rush to forgive always.
be thankful in all circumstances.
never be afraid to stand up for the truth, even if it hurts.
remember that heaven is our home.

YOUR FAMILY MISSION STATEMENT

Most of us associate mission statements with churches or businesses—not our personal relationships—and few of us have ever been in charge of developing them. To make the process easier, Jeanne Gowen Dennis and Focus on the Family posted a fill-in-the-blank guide in 2013 to help families get started envisioning, planning, and achieving their goals. You can find the guide at www.focusonthefamily.com/parenting/spiritual-growth-for-kids/writing-a-family-mission-statement. Give it a try!

He who gets wisdom loves his own soul;
he who keeps understanding will find good.

PROVERBS 19:8 NKJV

As we look to the future, not knowing where we may find ourselves or what situations we may encounter, one thing we are sure of is the need to have our lives continually rooted and grounded in the Lord. We are well aware there are areas where we both need growth. Our pride and preferences cause us to have silly spats and rub each other the wrong way. We know unattended love can grow cold, and we want ours to last until we reach the gates of heaven. There are sacrifices to be made, fallow ground in our hearts to be plowed (Hosea 10:12). There are seeds to be sown continually in order to reap a worthwhile harvest as the years go by.

A true relationship is when two people stick around to see the reward of their commitment.

We hope you feel a renewed vision and love for your marriage, but most importantly, we pray you fall in love with Jesus and invite Him into His rightful place in the center of your heart.

May you be enlightened—filled with wisdom and revelation—and may the Lord's hand rest mightily upon you and your marriage.

From our hearts to yours,
Jeremy and Adrienne

ACKNOWLEDGMENTS

A huge thank you to our publisher, Harvest House. We have loved working with everyone on the team. A special thanks to Bob Hawkins, Jr., for faithfully following what God laid on your heart.

Our editor, Kathleen Kerr, for your incredible encouragement and taking time to polish our manuscript.

Our cowriter, Amanda Hope Haley—thank you for being so encouraging and giving us bite-sized goals when the project was quite intimating initially. You make everything we say sound good. Your advice and contribution have been invaluable.

Faceout Studio—thank you for taking the time to brainstorm and create such a gorgeous cover and interior design! Your designs were so incredible, it was hard to choose a favorite.

Our manager, Matt Balm—there are no words for your friendship, Matty B. What a gift you have been to both of us. You, more than anyone, know the dynamics of "us" firsthand. Thank you for loving us so well and so faithfully.

Providential people—the Heitzigs for inviting us on one of the most memorable Israel trips ever and introducing us to Bob Hawkins. Who knew what would come from Bus #1? Jonathan Pitts, for giving Adrienne an opportunity to write for *For Girls Like You* and confirming how the Lord was working with the writing process and with Harvest House.

Our precious kids, Bella, Arie, and Egan—for understanding the long hours at the computer and who quickly quieted at the "Hold on a minute" signal, while it oftentimes ended up being much longer than that. Thank you for being so supportive of what we do and being engaged in our life together. We love you guys with all our hearts.

To our treasured inner circle, thank you for the refining conversations that have brought so much fruit in our lives. Thank you for loving us well and being speakers of truth.

Thank you to those who have supported us in various ways along the years. We don't take our platform lightly, and we're deeply thankful to be able to minister in the ways we do.

HTTPS://WWW.JEREMYCAMP.COM/

JEREMY @JEREMYCAMP
ADRIENNE @ADIEMUSIC

JEREMY @JEREMYCAMPOFFICIAL
ADRIENNE @ADIECAMP

JEREMY @JEREMYCAMP
ADRIENNE @ADIECAMP

ABOUT THE AUTHORS

Jeremy Camp is a GRAMMY®-nominated singer and songwriter who met his wife Adrienne, a South African singer and songwriter, while on tour. Jeremy and Adie have been married for 17 years and are passionate about keeping Jesus in the middle of their life and marriage and sharing God's love around the world in any way they can. They founded a non-profit together called "Speaking Louder Ministries" in efforts to share help and hope all across the globe.

Adrienne Camp is a South African singer and songwriter. She was the lead singer of the Christian rock band The Benjamin Gate and later recorded two solo albums. She is married to fellow musician Jeremy Camp. She and Jeremy have two daughters, Isabella and Arianne, and one son, Egan. She is also the author of children's book *Even Me*, as well as a contributor to *For Girls Like You* magazine.

Amanda Hope Haley is a lover of the Bible—its God, its words, and its history. She is the author of *Mary Magdalene Never Wore Blue Eye Shadow: How to Trust the Bible When Truth and Tradition Collide*. She also hosts *The Red-Haired Archaeologist* podcast and contributed to The Voice Bible translation. Amanda holds a master's degree of theological studies in Hebrew Scripture and interpretation from Harvard University. She and her husband, David, live in Tennessee with their always-entertaining basset hound, Copper.

www.amandahopehaley.com

NOTES

Chapter 1

[1] Søren Kierkegaard, journal entry, July 7, 1838, in *The Soul of Kierkegaard: Selections from His Journal*, ed. Alexander Dru (Mineola, NY: Dover, 2003), 59.

[2] "Difference Between Covenant and Contract," *UpCounsel*, accessed April 30, 2019, http://www.upcounsel.com/difference-between-covenant-and-contract.

Chapter 2

[1] Philip Yancey, *Vanishing Grace: What Ever Happened to the Good News?* (Grand Rapids, MI: Zondervan, 2014), 33.

[2] Tim and Joy Downs, *Fight Fair! Winning at Conflict Without Losing at Love* (Chicago: Moody, 2003).

Chapter 3

[1] Oswald Chambers, "August 28: The Purpose of Prayer," *The Golden Book of Oswald Chambers: My Utmost for His Highest; Selections for the Year* (New York: Dodd, Mead and Company, 1935), 241.

[2] Adapted from Bette Morgan's "Praying for Your Husband," *Just Between Us*, accessed July 15, 2019, justbetweenus.org/ministry/pastors-wives/praying-for-your-husband.

Chapter 4

[1] Vince Vitale, "If God, Why Suffering?" *RZIM*, accessed June 17, 2019, http://www.rzim.org/read/just-thinking-magazine/if-god-why-suffering.

[2] Elisabeth Kübler-Ross, *On Death and Dying* (New York: Simon and Schuster, 1969).

[3] David B. Feldman, "Why the Five Stages of Grief Are Wrong," *Psychology Today* (blog), July 7, 2017, http://www.psychologytoday.com/us/blog/supersurvivors/201707/why-the-five-stages-grief-are-wrong.

[4] Vince Vitale, "A Response of Hope," in Ravi Zacharias and Vince Vitale, *Why Suffering? Finding Meaning and Comfort When Life Doesn't Make Sense* (New York: FaithWords, 2014), 191.

Chapter 5

[1] Lea Winerman, "By the Numbers: Antidepressant Use on the Rise," American Psychological Association, *Monitor on Psychology* 48, no. 10 (November 2017): 120, http://www.apa.org/monitor/2017/11/numbers.

[2] Neil T. Anderson and Rich Miller, *Freedom from Fear: Overcoming Worry and Anxiety* (Eugene, OR: Harvest House, 1999), 19.

[3] F.B. Meyer, as quoted in Sherwood Eliot Wirt and Kersten Beckstrom, eds., *Living Quotations for Christians* (New York: Harper and Row, 1974), 76.

[4] "Mental Illness," National Institute of Mental Health, US Department of Health and Human Services, last modified February 2019, http://www.nimh.nih.gov/health/statistics/mental-illness.shtml.

[5] Elisabeth Elliot, *Keep a Quiet Heart* (Ann Arbor, MI: Servant, 1995), 20.

[6] Philip Yancey, *Prayer: Does It Make Any Difference?* (Grand Rapids, MI: Zondervan, 2006), 303.

[7] Timothy Keller with Kathy Keller, *The Meaning of Marriage: Facing the Complexities of Commitment with the Wisdom of God* (New York: Penguin, 2013), 132.

Chapter 6

[1] Dave Ramsey, "Marriage, Money, and Communication," February 7, 2018, https://www.daveramsey.com/research/money-marriage-communication; Ramsey Solutions, "Money Ruining Marriages in America: A Ramsey Solutions Study," February 7, 2018, https://www.daveramsey.com/pr/money-ruining-marriages-in-america.

[2] "Millennials Making Financial Progress, but Efforts Thwarted by Influence of Social Media," *Allianz*, February 6, 2018, http://www.allianzlife.com/about/news-and-events/news-releases/Millennials-Generations-Ahead-study.

[3] "Average US Credit Card Debt in 2019," *MagnifyMoney* (blog), March 26, 2019, http://www.magnifymoney.com/blog/news/u-s-credit-card-debt-by-the-numbers628618371.

[4] Rachel Layne, "The Skyrocketing Interest Payments on US Debt," *MoneyWatch*, CBS News, October 11, 2018, http://www.cbsnews.com/news/the-skyrocketing-interest-payments-on-u-s-debt.

[5] "Scholarship for a Girl to Attend Secondary School, Catalog Number 0206," *CARE*, accessed May 15, 2019, http://gifts.care.org/education/scholarship-for-a-girl-to-attend-secondary-school.

[6] "What's the Cost," *Water Wells for Africa*, accessed May 15, 2019, http://waterwellsforafrica.org/whats-the-cost.

[7] Matthew Nitch Smith, "The 19 Most Expensive Buildings Ever Constructed," *Business Insider*, May 27, 2016, http://www.businessinsider.com/the-most-expensive-buildings-ever-adjusted-for-inflation.

[8] Maher Chmaytelli and Ahmed Hagagy, "Iraq Says Reconstruction After War on Islamic State to Cost $88 Billion," *Reuters*, February 12, 2018, http://www.reuters.com/article/us-mideast-crisis-iraq-reconstruction/iraq-says-reconstruction-after-war-on-islamic-state-to-cost-88-billion-idUSKBN1FW0JB.

[9] According to estimated costs from 2015; "Economic Impact of Cancer," *American Cancer Society*, last modified January 3, 2018, http://www.cancer.org/cancer/cancer-basics/economic-impact-of-cancer.html.

[10] According to estimates from 2019; Connor Harrison, "How Much Is a Mother Really Worth?" *Salary.com*, May 10, 2019, http://www.salary.com/articles/mother-salary.

Chapter 7

[1] Wynter Pitts and Jonathan Pitts, *Emptied: Experiencing the Fullness of a Poured-Out Marriage* (Eugene, OR: Harvest House, 2019), 46.

[2] John Newton to Mary Catlett, Olney, July 21, 1764, in *The Works of the Rev. John Newton*, vol. 4 (New Haven: Nathan Whiting, 1826), 161.

Chapter 8

[1] Ogden Nash, *Marriage Lines: Notes of a Student Husband* (New York: Little, Brown and Company, 1964), 79.

[2] Robert C. Dodds, *Two Together: A Handbook for Your Marriage* (New York: Thomas Y. Crowell, 1959), 95.

Chapter 9

[1] Chantal Bechervaise, "5 Reasons Why Vision Is Important in Leadership," *Take It Personel-ly* (blog), October 14, 2013, http://takeitpersonelly .com/2013/10/14/5-reasons-why-vision-is-important-in-leadership.

[2] George MacDonald, *The Miracles of Our Lord* (London: Strahan and Company, 1870), 126.

[3] Natasha Crain, *Talking with Your Kids About God: 30 Conversations Every Christian Parent Must Have* (Grand Rapids, MI: Baker, 2017), 229.

[4] "The Insufficiency of Reason as a Substitute for Revelation," in *The Works of Jonathan Edwards, A. M.*, ed. Edward Hickman (London: William Ball, 1839), 2:479-85.

Chapter 10

[1] Philip Yancey, *What's So Amazing About Grace?* (Grand Rapids, MI: Zondervan, 1997), 34-37,70-73.

Chapter 11

1 Keller, *Meaning of Marriage*, 9.

2 Thomas Chalmers, *The Expulsive Power of a New Affection: A Sermon* (London: Hatchard and Company, 1861), 11.

3 H.S. Holland, *Creed and Character: Sermons* (London: Rivingtons, 1887), 294-295.

4 Lewis B. Smedes, *Standing on the Promises: Keeping Hope Alive for a Tomorrow We Cannot Control* (Nashville, TN: Thomas Nelson, 1998), 109.

5 Corrie ten Boom with Jamie Buckingham, *Tramp for the Lord: The Story That Begins Where* The Hiding Place *Ends* (Fort Washington, PA: CLC, 2011), 183,57.

6 Amy Carmichael, "Make Me Thy Fuel" in *Toward Jerusalem: Poems of Faith* (London: SPCK, 1936), 94.

M

Look for other great
Harvest House books at

WWW.HARVESTHOUSEPUBLISHERS.COM